DR. JOHN F. WALVOORD

JOHN F. WALVOORD is President of
Dallas Theological Seminary, and
Editor of *Bibliotheca Sacra*, America's
oldest theological quarterly, which is
published by Dallas Seminary.

Associated with Dr. Lewis Sperry
Chafer in teaching and administration
at Dallas Seminary for more than fif-
teen years, Dr. Walvoord was chosen
to succeed the founder of the school
upon his death in 1952.

A graduate of Wheaton College
and Dallas Seminary, Dr. Walvoord
holds the A.M. degree from Texas
Christian University in philosophy
and the Th.D. degree from Dallas
Seminary in Systematic Theology.

THE RETURN OF THE LORD

The Return of the Lord

by

JOHN F. WALVOORD, Th.D.

President, Dallas Theological Seminary,
Dallas, Texas

———

DUNHAM PUBLISHING COMPANY
GRAND RAPIDS, MICHIGAN 49506

PREFACE

Few statements have ever been uttered more dramatic and more significant than the simple words of our Lord, "I will come again." Gathered in this prediction is a whole system of Christian faith, a profound philosophy of history, a guiding star for Christian hope. Here for the believer is the assurance of deathless life, of the ultimate triumph of righteousness, of rest and peace, joy and fellowship, of endless glory in the presence of God.

Our generation theologically is characterized by renewed emphasis upon future things. The world is in a state of expectancy and a key to the future is widely sought. In such a context, the present series of messages is made available in written form in the expectation of providing light and hope for believers in Christ. Each chapter is designed to be sufficient in itself while contributing to Christian doctrine as a whole. For the most part, the truth is presented in popular sermonic form much as it was preached.

Acknowledgment is made for permission to reprint with revision Chapter I from *King's Business,* Chapter IV and Chapter X from *Eternity* Magazine, Chapter VI from *Christian Life* Magazine, and Chapters V, VII, and VIII from *Bibliotheca Sacra.* The remaining chapters are being published for the first time. Subjects selected for publication in this volume are focused upon the return of the Lord, and if in some measure this truth is magnified and His name glorified the human author will be grateful.

July, 1955   JOHN F. WALVOORD

CONTENTS

7

CHAPTER I

TRENDS OF OUR DAY TOWARD
FULFILLMENT OF PROPHECY

THE APPROACHING END OF THE AGE

THE WHOLE world is in a state of fearful expectation. The advent of the atomic bomb with kindred devastating weapons has brought the world face to face with the possibility of the doom of present civilization. It is a matter of common discussion and much literature whether the world's population faces annihilation and, if not, whether the destructive forces let loose by war will not in any event destroy civilization to the extent that it will lose its present character. To a Christian who accepts the Bible as the Word of God such questions are not merely academic, but rather point to the Biblical question of whether we are approaching the end of the present age.

THE BIBLICAL PICTURE OF THE FUTURE

Students of the Bible have long studied the Biblical pattern of future events. For those who interpret the Bible literally, this has yielded a definite program for the future. According to the Scriptures, the Lord Jesus Christ will return to meet His church in the air. Following this event, while the church is in heaven, a world government will come into being. In its early stages the political leader of this government will enter into a covenant with Israel providing for Israel's protection and liberty in their native land of Palestine (Dan. 9:27). As the world government

9

becomes stronger and comes to the peak of its power, absolute control is exercised over the press, business, and religion as well as the political sovereignty of the states in the world government (Rev. 13:7-8, 16-17). The political head will be a dictator of tremendous power who will deify himself (Rev. 13:8). All will be required to worship him and Jews and Christians who resist this order will be put to death in great number (Rev. 7:9-17; 13:7-8, 15). Simultaneous with these events will be a series of great catastrophic judgments which God will pour out on the earth which will destroy most of the earth's population (Rev. 6—19). The political movement of the time will culminate in a tremendous world war with Palestine as its vortex. As the world's armies converge on Israel's ancient land, the Lord will return from heaven with the church and the holy angels to judge the world in righteousness and to destroy all the wicked. Such a sequence of events has never occurred in the history of the world and will be easily recognizable when it takes place. As the coming of the Lord for His church precedes the fulfillment of these prophecies, we need not look for their fulfillment now. The significance of world events in the light of these prophecies is that we can see in our day preparation on a colossal scale for just such a period. The trends of our time toward the fulfillment of prophecy sound a clarion call to attention. The march of these stirring events is about to begin.

Three Lines of Evidence

The Apostle Paul, writing by inspiration, furnishes a divinely authorized division of the peoples of the earth when he refers to the Jews, Gentiles, and the church of God (1 Cor. 10:32). Here is distinguished the purpose of God in these three categories, concerning each of which the Scriptures speak much in detail. During this age the Jews are in dispersion, persecuted, blinded, wandering. This is in fulfillment of many prophecies of the Old and New Testament (cf. Deut. 28:58-68; Rom. 11). For the Gentiles this is the time of power and blessing. To Gentiles the gospel is freely offered. To Gentiles is given political power and wealth. It is still the times of the Gentiles begun in 600 B.C. and the time of the fullness of the Gentiles begun at Pentecost. It is also the time of the formation of the church of God of both Jew and Gentile. In this age God is calling out a people for His name. An examination of these three lines of revelation will unfold a marvelous movement of God in our day. The evidence points to the conclusion that the present age is fast running its course.

THE STATE OF THE CHURCH

The Scriptures speak not only of the church as the body of Christ but also as a sphere of profession, including many who are not actually saved. In this sphere of profession the Scriptures predict a fearful apostasy and turning away from the truth during the present age. According to 1 Timothy 4:1, "some shall depart from the faith," and the characteristics of these as defined in this passage are easily found in the world. Peter predicts the coming of false prophets "who privily shall bring in damnable heresies, even denying the Lord that bought them" (2 Pet. 2:1). One of the most obvious heresies of our day within the professing church is the denial that the sacrifice and shed blood of Christ "bought" us and constituted an actual redemption. Liberals object to such hymns as "Jesus Paid It All" as outmoded theology and contrary to their doctrine that God loves everybody. No point will bring withering scorn among liberals like the Biblical teaching on the blood of Christ. These prophecies concerning false teachers have all been fulfilled in our day.

Peter concludes his extended section (2 Pet. 2:1—3:18) on

apostasy with a prediction that unbelievers will scoff at the doctrine of the second coming: "Knowing this first, that there shall come in the last days scoffers, walking after their own lusts, and saying, Where is the promise of his coming? for since the fathers fell asleep, all things continue as they were from the beginning of the creation" (2 Pet. 3:3-4). One of the most evident facts of modern Christianity is that liberals do not preach the second coming of Christ. The great mass of church-going, professing Christians are ignorant of the simple elements of the doctrine of the second coming because they have been robbed of it by an unbelieving leadership. The doctrine of the second coming of Christ and its accompanying teaching of judgment upon sin is not palatable to modern rejectors of the truth of God. The precise form of opposition anticipated in the Bible nineteen hundred years ago is found in contemporary theology as never before in the history of the age. An examination of these and many other prophecies concerning the course of the church in the world will impress one with the fact that every prophecy concerning the church in the world has been fulfilled except the resurrection and translation of the true church, which events close the age, and the divine judgment on the apostate church which occurs later in the great tribulation. As far as the church is concerned, the trends of prophecy point to the imminency of the consummation, the glad moment when Christ will come for His own, the dead in Christ being raised and living believers translated into His glorious presence.

THE STATE OF THE WORLD

The state of the world, like the state of the church, is in the climactic stage. The frantic scramble to find a solution to the problem of the atomic bomb, the obvious disaster which faces much of civilization in the event of another world war, the disintegration of moral standards among nations, the impending clash of races and ideologies, and the growth of crime and cruelty combine to pose a problem of formidable proportions. These factors in their general character foreshadow unmistakably the apocalyptic events predicted for the tribulation.

In the world at large the rise of Russia as a great military power is a pointed fact. The prophecy of Ezekiel 38—39 has long been associated with Russia and the passage states expressly that the military invasion which sweeps upon Palestine comes from the north (Ezek. 38:15-16). While this maneuver is not dated in Scripture, it seems to be related to the events which close the age. It may well be that the Lord will come for His church before the invasion. The strategic position of Palestine astride the route from Europe to Asia, the tremendous oil reserves in that portion of the world, and the astronomical value of mineral deposits in Palestine all make it a unique prize. The rise of Russia certainly fits into the larger picture of the close of the age with amazing precision.

Coupled with Russia in our time is the incomputable military strength of the Orient. According to the Scriptures, one of the major elements in the final great battle which culminates in the return of the Lord to establish His kingdom on earth is the invasion from the east. A great army of two hundred million are pictured in Revelation 9:16 as related to the release of the angels bound in the River Euphrates to the east. Revelation 16:12 discloses that the way of the kings of the east, the leaders of the great Oriental army, is prepared by the drying up of that river. The convergence of this tremendous army upon Palestine is a preparation for Armageddon. The kings of the whole earth are "gathered" for "the battle of that great day of God Almighty" (Rev. 16:14). Never before in the history of the world has such an invasion been a greater probability. The moving of such a force overland to Palestine is possible in our day of mechanization as never before. The linking of the Orient with Russia is an alliance little dreamed of outside the Scriptures, but today this has become already a fearful reality.

Among the other phenomena of the present day which are of striking significance to the student of prophecy is the rise of atheism and the worship of power. For the first time in the history of the world a modern nation, Russia, has officially embraced atheism as its belief. Never on such a comprehensive scale has there been an organized attempt of this magnitude to erase every vestige of religion whether true or false. This has significance particularly as compared with the apostate religion which will characterize the time of the great tribulation. According to Daniel 11:38, the world leader will "honour the God of forces," or, as it is stated in the R.S.V. and A.S.V., "the God of fortresses." The god of apostasy will be the god of power, the personification of military might. With its roots in atheism and its utter blasphemy of the true God, modern Russia is the prototype of that which is to come. Already its subtle, God-defying philosophy has permeated the world and awaits the release which will come when the restraint of the Holy Spirit is lifted at the translation of the church.

Probably the most obvious feature of our day in the light of prophecy is the United Nations. For the first time there has been a workable union in which the great nations of the world have participated actively. In view of the predicted world government of the tribulation time (Rev. 13), the trend in our day toward centralization of power and the popular acceptance of world government as the way out of world chaos is of great importance. The man on the street, as well as the statesman in his secret councils, is looking for some sort of international agreement which will dissolve the tensions now existing and pave the way for world peace. Such a movement of minds and nations is the foreshadowing of the acceptance of the world government of the tribulation time and the bowing of the knee to the world dictator of that day as the unifying personality.

In the world today we can see, then, a portent of the gathering storm. The military might of Russia and the Orient is already a reality. The rise of atheism and of world government are already upon us. Never in the history of the world has there been such a converging of more ominous tokens that the climax is not far distant. For the Christian this is a divine sign that the day of deliverance is at hand.

THE STATE OF ISRAEL

From the time of Abraham the state of Israel has been an important barometer of the movements of God upon the pages of human history. The comparatively dormant state of Israel during so many centuries, with no noticeable progress in the fulfillment of her destiny, stands in contrast to the twentieth century. In the plan of God the Jew has been preserved through the captivities of the Old Testament and the dispersion of the New. Persecuted and hounded in most nations of the world, and subject in our generation to the most awful pogroms of her entire history, Israel today is a people being formed anew as a component of political society. Before World War I less than fifty thousand Jews lived in their ancient land of Palestine. Before World War II there were spasmodic attempts to repopulate Palestine. Since World War II there has been a swelling tide of immigrants. Returning at the rate of more than a hundred thousand a year, the present report is that 1,800,000 Jews are now living in Palestine. Never since the time of Moses has there been such a movement back to the land of their fathers. Not only have the numbers swelled, but a political state of Israel has been formed and recognized by the nations of the world who are friendly to the Jew.

For long years students of prophecy have predicted the return of the Jew to Palestine. Before World War I this interpretation was rejected by some who abruptly pointed to the opposition of the Turks to such a scheme. After World War I and even World War II opposition persisted to their return, but legally or illegally the movement continued.

As all students of prophecy know, the precise world conditions immediately after the coming of the Lord for the church anticipated that Israel would be in Palestine in sufficient numbers to be a recognizable political entity. With them the world leader would form a covenant (Dan. 9:27) and their ancient sacrifices would be reintroduced. Before World War I this would have been almost impossible, and prior to World War II this would have been improbable. But the formation of the State of Israel and the influx of pilgrims make the plausibility of such a covenant evident to anyone. In other words, in our day, and more precisely in the last ten years, there has been a movement of God among Israel which has set the stage as never before for exactly that fulfillment which is predicted for the period immediately after the translation of the church. We can even observe in our present world situation the tensions between Israel and Russia and the Orient which are seen in Scripture for the tribulation time. More prophecies have either been fulfilled or prepared for fulfillment in our day than in all the previous centuries since the first of our era.

The converging trend of fulfilled prophecy and preparation for fulfillment in the three areas of the church, the Gentiles, and the Jew point in the same direction. It is most obvious to conclude that we may expect the Lord momentarily. While the absence of some of these factors was not of sufficient importance to dim the hope of saints in centuries past for the imminent return of the Lord, the presence of these significant omens should surely strengthen our hope. The preparation for the final drama is being carried on before our eyes.

THE CHALLENGE OF THE HOUR

The revelation of the prophetic Word was not designed simply to comfort and to enlighten. The hope of the Lord's return should constitute an impelling challenge. The task is large and the days are few. It is time for searching of heart and purification of life. It is time for prayer and devotion, for sacrifice and effort. Now is the time to preach the good news of a Savior who died for the sins of the whole world that all who believe might live. It is a time to press on through closing missionary doors, through opposition, unbelief, and indifference. It is time to remind ourselves of that searching evaluation of our life and labors that awaits us at the judgment seat of Christ. The coming of the Lord is as near as our next breath, the next beat of our hearts, the next word of our lips. While we wait, may we be "stedfast, unmoveable, always abounding in the work of the Lord" (1 Cor. 15:58).

CHAPTER II

A PREMILLENNIAL CALENDAR
OF FUTURE EVENTS

A GENUINE Christian point of view in considering the past or the future is that God is unfolding an intelligent purpose in human events. History, while not always understood, is the outworking of this sovereign purpose of a sovereign God. There are no accidents in history. The same God who ordained that history would take place as it has and unfold its tremendous revelation of God and His dealings with creation, has also the ability to prewrite history and give us what we call prophecy.

The age in which we live is sensing that it is moving forward to some sort of goal. There is no clear voice among the wise men of our day, however, to tell us where we are going. The reason why men do not know and cannot tell is that they have neglected the only Book in all the world which will tell us accurately and without error concerning future events. The Bible has demonstrated by fulfilled prophecy over thousands of years that it predicts accurately and literally. This has been proved by hundreds of fulfilled prophecies which have already taken place. Because of this assurance, we can come to the Word of God with the same confidence that future events will take place according to the revealed will of God as we have concerning the record of history which has already been fulfilled.

If the Bible is read from Genesis to Revelation with special attention to prophecies which have not been fulfilled, it will be found that they number into the thousands. It is possible, how-

ever, to arrange these prophecies in a simple outline of eight
major divisions.

THE CALENDAR FOR THE PRESENT AGE

The Word of God provides, first of all, a revelation concerning the present age. One of the reasons for confusion concerning future events is the failure to analyze correctly the purpose
of God in this present age. Some have come to the Bible without
a proper method of interpretation. The premillennial return
of Christ contains many important doctrines, but it also provides
the key to unlock the prophetic Word. One of the reasons for
failure to understand God's program of events is that some have
tried a key other than the great truth of the premillennial return
of Christ. This is true particularly of the meaning and purpose
of God in this present age. The amillenarian, who denies that
there will be a future millennium or kingdom reign of Christ
on earth, tries to find in the *present* age the fulfillment of God's
purpose to establish a righteous kingdom on earth. He is therefore obligated to find some explanation of the many chapters
in the Old Testament which picture a period of righteousness
and peace and of justice in the earth. Because this is so obviously
not true, amillenarians have been forced, particularly in recent
generations, to spiritualize the Scripture to the point where they
have taken these prophecies as a picture of heaven or the inter-
mediate state. With such a system of interpretation, there is
not only no key to the future but there is also no key to the
present. The premillennial point of view, assumed here, permits
an intelligent understanding of what God is doing in the present age.

According to the revelation of Scripture, there are three
aspects of the present age which are prominent in the prophetic
portrayal of this age. First, it is revealed in Scripture that it is

the purpose of God in this present age to gather out from both
Jew and Gentile a people called the church, the body and bride of
Christ. In Matthew 16:18 there is a declaration of this purpose
from the lips of Christ. He said to Peter, "Thou art Peter, and
upon this rock I will build my church." Those last five words
are emphatic. "I" speaks of Christ as the One who will fulfill
the prophecies. "Will" indicates a future work in distinction
to what God has done in the past. "Build" implies a process,
something not accomplished in a moment, but spread over the
age. "My" makes clear that the church is the personal possession
of Christ. The word "church," which comes from a Greek
word meaning *to call out,* speaks of the present purpose of God
in calling out from Jew and Gentile those who will trust in
Jesus Christ as Savior. These called-out ones, being baptized
by the Holy Spirit into the body of Christ, form a new entity, a
saved people, an organism united by life to Christ at its head.

In Ephesians 5:25-27 this purpose is stated in simple and
wonderful words, given in connection with instruction to hus-
bands:

> "Husbands, love your wives, even as Christ also loved the
> church, and gave himself for it; that he might sanctify and
> cleanse it with the washing of water by the word, that he
> might present it to himself a glorious church, not having
> spot, or wrinkle, or any such thing; but that it should be
> holy and without blemish."

It is God's purpose to take Jew and Gentile alike, sanctify
them by the Holy Spirit and by the blood of Christ, and form
them into His church. Eventually, as the Scriptures anticipate,
He will present them to Himself as a bride which is spotless, a
glorious church, not having spot or wrinkle or any such thing,
but holy and without blemish. This purpose of God is in the

process of being fulfilled. It will come to its climax when Christ comes for His church and takes His church home to heaven.

Along with this purpose of calling out a church, a second aspect of the present age is revealed in Matthew 13, under the figure of the kingdom of heaven in its mystery form. This passage describes the progress of Christendom in its largest meaning. The wheat and the tares will grow up together, representing those who are truly saved and those who seem to be saved but who are not. Both continue until the harvest. In the parables in Matthew 13 Christendom is likened to the mustard seed, which with a small beginning grows into a great tree. Organized Christianity—Protestant, Roman, and Greek together —has grown into a tremendous tree, something which all the world recognizes, but this is not synonymous to the church which is the body of Christ. It is the professing church; it is Christendom; it is the kingdom of heaven in its mystery form.

The Scriptures also make plain that another characteristic of the professing church is its growing apostasy, its utter departure from God as it reaches its climax. Second Timothy 3:13 states: "But evil men and seducers shall wax worse and worse, deceiving, and being deceived." Therefore we have, first of all, in the present age the calling out of the church, the body of Christ, and, second, we have the organization of Christendom growing to tremendous proportions, but in the process traveling the road to utter apostasy. A third aspect which is revealed in Scripture concerning the present age is that it will be characterized by war, by pestilence, by earthquake, and by wickedness. In other words, the Gentile world as a whole is going to be continually in turmoil. The Scriptures anticipate that at the close of the period it will grow worse and worse until finally it ends in the great tribulation preceding Christ's coming to establish His kingdom. The Bible has, then, a very specific program or calendar of events for this present age.

NEXT EVENT: THE IMMINENT TRANSLATION OF THE CHURCH

When this present age has about run its course, the translation of the church will abruptly bring the church age to a close. In this major event, there are four parts. In 1 Thessalonians 4 it is revealed that at the time of this event the dead in Christ will be raised. The very moment following this, the translation of the church will occur, which is described not only in 1 Thessalonians 4 but more specifically in 1 Corinthians 15:51-52. There we are told that in a moment, in the twinkling of an eye, we will be changed from these mortal bodies to immortal bodies and from corruptible bodies to incorruptible bodies. The dead in Christ will rise first, and Christians living in the world at that time will be transformed in a moment of time and caught up with them to meet the Lord in the air.

The Scriptures also reveal that when this event takes place we will go home to heaven. John 14:3 records that when Christ was leaving His disciples He told them, "I will come again, and receive you unto myself; that where I am, there ye may be also." The promise is that when we meet Christ in the air He will take us home to the Father's house, another expression for heaven, where Christ is now preparing a place for us.

Following this there is a fourth event, the judgment seat of Christ, pictured in 2 Corinthians 5:10-11 and 1 Corinthians 3:11-15, describing the event in heaven when we appear before Christ and receive our rewards. In connection with this, we are joined to Christ in the marriage of the Lamb, which could be regarded as another event. When Christ comes for His church, there unfolds for us who are Christians this sequence of tremendous events which are a part of our intelligent Christian hope.

THE SEVENTIETH WEEK OF DANIEL AND THE SECOND COMING

While these events are taking place in heaven, there is another series of events which are taking place on earth and which make up the third major division in the program of God in the future calendar of events. That series of events is the fulfillment of the seventieth week of Daniel's program for Israel climaxing with the second coming of Christ. In a word, it is the fulfillment of Daniel 9:27 which predicts that there is yet ahead a period of seven years of human history on earth which will begin with a covenant between the Gentile world ruler and the Jewish people. Palestine is set apart as the national home for Israel, where Jews are protected and sheltered. This enables Israel to re-establish their ancient sacrifices. This will be cut short by the beginning of the great tribulation and the breaking of the covenant with the Jews, with the result that Israel becomes the object of persecution and wrath instead of being protected.

Along with this program for Israel, the Scriptures reveal that tremendous events will take place in the earth. In that period of time the great prophecy of Ezekiel 38—39, predicting a military invasion from Russia of the land of Palestine, will probably take place. There will be other great military conflicts. Out of it will come a world government with a world dictator accompanied by a world religious ruler, both of whom are clearly described in Revelation 13. The whole world will be united in one world government ruled by this evil character who, according to Scripture, is a blasphemer of God and who sets himself up as God.

The last three and a half years of this seven-year program will be the time of Jacob's trouble and the time of great tribulation. It is a time of trouble such as this world has never even dreamed of to this hour, apart from the revelation of the Word of God. At the conclusion of this period, the Scriptures indicate that Christ is coming back in power and great glory. The heavens will be ablaze with glory when He comes to establish His kingdom on earth.

JUDGMENT OF LIVING GENTILES

The fourth great prophetic event in the divine calendar of the future is the judgment of the Gentiles. In Matthew 25:31-46 the Gentiles are gathered and judged by God. These are not resurrected ones, but living Gentiles who have come through the time of tribulation and now are being judged by Christ in relation to their fitness for entrance into the millennial kingdom of righteousness and peace. The separation of the sheep from the goats takes place and the sheep are ushered into the kingdom. The goats, those unworthy, are cast into everlasting fire. The basis of this judgment is the treatment given "my brethren," the Jews. In the tribulation, no one except a believer in Christ will befriend the Jews. Accordingly, kindness to the Jews becomes an evidence of salvation by faith.

REGATHERING AND JUDGMENT OF ISRAEL

A fifth event described in Ezekiel 20:34-38 is the judgment of Israel. The regathering of Israel has already begun in our present generation. Over 1,800,000 Jews are now in Palestine. More than ten percent of all the Jews in the world have gone back to the land of Palestine. This process of regathering is going to be continued after Christ comes for His church and will proceed during the first three and one-half years of that seven-year period prophesied by Daniel. This regathering will be abruptly stopped at the beginning of the great tribulation.

When Christ comes back, one of the things He accomplishes at the beginning of His millennial reign is the completion of the task of bringing all the Jews back to the place where He will judge them. Ezekiel 20:38 says that He is going to purge out the rebels of Israel which is a purging out of the unbelievers from among those who in the dark hours of the tribulation time turned to Christ as their Messiah and their Savior. This godly remnant who welcomed Him when He came back will be ushered into the millennial kingdom and into the land which was promised their fathers.

The Millennial Reign of Christ

The sixth division of the divine calendar is the millennial reign of Christ itself. In Revelation 20:4-6, it is disclosed very specifically that this is going to be a period of one thousand years beginning at the return of Christ and ending with some very specific events. The Scriptures declare that during this time Satan will be bound. All demonic activity will cease in that time, and for the first time in all the history of the human race man will be without any satanic temptation. Any evil which arises must arise in that time from the heart of man alone. Christ will reign over this world and there will be righteousness, peace, and justice. There will be joy in the earth and prosperity in economic things.

The Final Judgment at the Great White Throne

At the close of the millennium there will be a seventh great event in God's calendar: the final rebellion and the judgment of the great white throne. Scripture indicates that Satan will be loosed from his binding and he will be permitted once again to deceive the nations. As he goes forth to deceive the nations, a great horde of the human population from those who are born on the earth during the millennium—who merely professed to follow Christ without ever having been really born again—will follow Satan and be deceived by him. The Scriptures state that fire will come from heaven and devour them. The millennial earth and the present heaven will be destroyed, and a new heaven and a new earth will be created. Before the new heaven and new earth are created, the judgment of the great white throne, described in Revelation 20:11-15, will take place. Christ will bring into judgment every unsaved soul, and everyone who does not have eternal life—whose name is not written in the Lamb's book of life—will be cast into the lake of fire.

CREATION OF NEW HEAVENS AND NEW EARTH

The great climactic event, the creation of the new heavens and the new earth (Rev. 21:1), follows immediately the final judgment, beginning what Peter seems to refer to as the Day of God (2 Pet. 3:12), the eternity which stretches on without end, concerning which we have no detailed program revealed in the Scripture.

The prophetic program of Scripture emphasizes the urgency to receive Christ and to trust Him for Salvation. We need the assurance that our part in that program will be that of one who has trusted in Christ, who is a member of the body of Christ, bound for glory.

If this calendar of events is true, it also emphasizes the responsibility of every child of God to spend the moments, the strength, and the opportunities which God gives in a way that is profitable from the standpoint of eternity. One of these days all of us will stand before Christ in judgment. The question which will be raised at that time is: "What have you done with the gospel message, with the life I have given you, with the substance, with the time, with the opportunity, with the spiritual gifts with which you are endowed?" Paul speaks of the terror of the Lord in 2 Corinthians 5:11 as he contemplates the possibility of being one for whom Christ died, one who claimed the grace of God, and who is cleansed by the precious blood, and yet with a wasted life, a lost opportunity, a life that has not been spent intelligently in relation to God's prophetic calendar of events. As we study the stupendous program which God has before us, may our hearts be challenged to make every day count for our Savior, living with the divine calendar of future events guiding our steps.

Chapter III

IS THE RETURN OF CHRIST
PREMILLENNIAL?

Prophecy a Biblical Study

THOSE WHO have studied prophecy as a whole will realize that the subject of the premillennial return of Christ is much too vast to complete in one chapter. It is possible, however, to give a summary of the essential facts of this tremendous doctrine.

Some today are saying that it does not make much difference what we believe about the coming of the Lord and that the emphasis on the premillennial return of Christ is a misguided effort. They urge that we concentrate on inspiring Christians to win others to know Christ as Savior, and to experience a deeper spiritual life; that we emphasize present spiritual issues and let the future take care of itself.

All thinking Christians will agree that it is possible to put too much time on any one phase of truth, including the prophetic word. A few may be guilty of studying prophecy without facing the challenge of living for Christ and bearing a real testimony for Him. The Word of God itself, however, gives us teaching on the proper place of prophetic study. While it places a great emphasis on the gospel and on living for Christ in the present, it also contains much about the future. Certainly God knew what He was doing when He guided the men who penned the Scriptures to write about prophecy. So in studying the subject of the coming of the Lord, we are simply doing that which the Scriptures do. The study of the premillennial return of Christ will help one to see the significance of many present world events, as well as something of the prospects that are before the Christian.

Not all students of Scripture agree on the exact place of the return of the Lord in the prophetic program. In general there are three different answers given, regarding the time of the coming of Christ. These are commonly described as the postmil-lennial, amillennial, and premillennial views. If the teaching involved in these terms is understood, it will enable one to understand some of the reasons why there is such confusion in much of the Biblical teaching of our day. Only one of these three ways is in agreement with the Scriptures. Anyone who wants to study the Bible and be instructed must face the issues and come to a conclusion about it.

POSTMILLENNIAL THEORY OF THE LORD'S RETURN

First of all, what do we mean by the postmillennial return of Christ? About three hundred years ago there was a man by the name of Daniel Whitby who was a Unitarian and something of a heretic. In fact, his writings on the Trinity were publicly burned by the Church of England. He introduced a relatively new idea in prophetic teaching, that the gospel would be preached throughout the world with such increasing success that eventually the whole world would be Christianized, and that everyone would come in one sense or another to the knowledge of Christ. He thought that by means of preaching the gospel a Christian civili-zation would be realized throughout the world which would reach the level of universal peace and righteousness predicted by the prophets. He anticipated this time of peace and righteous-ness and blessing under the gospel would go on for a thousand years or a millennium of time (the word *millennium* means a thousand years). At the conclusion of that period, it was Whitby's belief that Christ would come back and hence His return would be postmillennial, or after the millennium.

This view became very popular in spite of the fact that it was introduced by a heretic. It was adopted by many orthodox people, and became the predominant concept about fifty years ago concerning Christ's return. When World War I started, however, people began to ask whether the gospel ever would conquer the whole world, and whether the world after all was getting better and better.

POSTMILLENNIALISM NOW DISCARDED

From a practical standpoint, the beginning of World War II destroyed the hope that the world would get better and better and eventually become Christianized.

For the most part, postmillennialism is a discarded theory today. The postmillennial interpretation of the Bible is not according to either the Bible or history. There is no evidence that the world is moving toward a universal acclaim of the Lord Jesus Christ. For all practical purposes, this view may be dismissed.

THE AMILLENNIAL VIEW

This leaves the two remaining views to be considered—amillennialism and premillennialism. Just what is meant by amillennialism? The letter *a* is a prefix added to indicate negative meaning. Amillennialism is a term that is given to the non-millennial view and properly represents the concept of those who deny that there ever will be a millennium or a thousand-year reign of Christ on the earth. It has quite a history which cannot be considered here. It was popularized by a Roman Catholic father by the name of Augustine who lived in the fourth and fifth centuries. He believed that the only millennium there ever would be was the millennium in which he was living. This began the popular belief that the millennium is this present age, between the first and second comings of Christ. Augustine, however, saw so much sin, paganism, unbelief, and opposition to God that he had to admit that there was not any universal peace or righteousness on the earth in his day. It certainly was obvious to anyone that the millennial conditions pictured in the Bible were not being fulfilled in any realistic sense. So Augustine spiritualized the prophecies dealing with the millennium and in effect did away with a literal fulfillment of them. That is why this view is known as the amillennial or nonmillennial position. According to this method of interpreting prophecy, when Christ comes back He will not introduce a millennium but, instead, will usher in the eternal state at once. If this view were true, there would be no thousand-year reign of Christ on the earth after His second coming.

THE PREMILLENNIAL VIEW

Opposed to this denial of the millennium is the premillennial view, which was the belief of the early church from the first century. This belief concerning the prophetic Scriptures has been commonly taught for many years in Bible conferences and held by many Bible teachers and Christian institutions. The premillennial position is, in a word, that Christ is coming back to the world before the establishment of the millennial kingdom. Many believe that Christ is coming back to take the church to heaven first. This will be followed by a time of great trouble in the world while the church is in heaven with the Lord. After this time of trouble, Christ will return to the earth with the church to establish His millennial kingdom. From the standpoint of the premillennial return, it means simply that when Christ comes back to establish His kingdom He will bring this world to a place of peace and righteousness by His power and presence. He will rule for a thousand years, and there will be the fulfillment of the promised kingdom on the earth of which Christ will be King. As absolute ruler, He will punish sin as He acts in perfect righteousness. There will be no open sin permitted and the whole world will be filled with the knowledge of the Lord. In other words, the idea of a premillennial return of Christ pictures Christ coming back first and after that the millennial age, the kingdom on earth, will follow, lasting for a thousand years.

IS THE MILLENNIAL AGE PRESENT OR FUTURE?

These three millennial views are quite different, and only one of them can be right. If one dismisses the postmillennial idea that a millennium will come through preaching the gospel, it leaves the question of choosing between amillennialism and premillennialism—whether the present age fulfills the millennium, as the amillennial view holds, or whether the millennium will be fulfilled in the future after Christ returns, as premillenarians believe. A study of the Scripture will present the fact that this present age is not a fulfillment of the promised kingdom. We are not in the millennium today in any real sense of the word. Therefore, if we believe the Bible to be the Word of God and interpret it in its ordinary literal sense, we must look forward to a future time when Christ Himself will bring the kingdom to pass after He returns.

THE PROMISE OF A NEW COVENANT FOR ISRAEL

The Scriptures abound in promises that God gave to the nation Israel concerning the future kingdom. In Jeremiah 31:31-34 there is a prophecy of a new covenant that God will make with

Israel. It will be in contrast to the covenant that He made through Moses to the children of Israel in Egypt. It is defined in these words:

> "But this shall be the covenant that I will make with the house of Israel; After those days, saith the LORD, I will put my law in their inward parts, and write it in their hearts; and will be their God, and they shall be my people. And they shall teach no more every man his neighbor, and every man his brother, saying, Know the LORD: for they shall all know me, from the least of them unto the greatest of them, saith the LORD: for I will forgive their iniquity, and I will remember their sin no more" (Jer. 31:33-34).

This passage predicts that there will be a future period in Israel's history when the knowledge of the Lord will be so universal that one will not have to be a missionary to his neighbor. It will not be necessary to distribute gospel tracts or to do any of the things that concern the extension of the gospel to the heathen. The Scripture prophesies that everyone will know the truth about the Lord in that day. They will know that He is the Son of God and the Messiah and the King of kings.

The Scriptures clearly predict that this will be true. Is it true today? It certainly is not true. One could canvass the situation in the very block in which he lives and find that there are many people who do not know anything about the Lord. There are those who do not know the difference between the Old and the New Testament. There is colossal ignorance concerning the Lord today. In that day, however, everyone will know the Lord for He will be the King of the whole earth.

THE PROMISE OF ISRAEL'S CONTINUANCE AS A NATION

The nation Israel is given additional promises in verses 35-37 which continue the passage just quoted:

"Thus saith the LORD, which giveth the sun for a light by day, and the ordinances of the moon and of the stars for a light by night, which divideth the sea when the waves thereof roar; The LORD of hosts is his name: if those ordinances depart from before me, saith the LORD, then the seed of Israel also shall cease from being a nation before me for ever. Thus saith the LORD; If heaven above can be measured, and the foundations of the earth searched out beneath, I will also cast off all the seed of Israel for all that they have done, saith the LORD" (Jer. 31:35-37).

What does this passage teach? It teaches that Israel as a nation will continue as long as the sun and moon endure. God declares that it is just as impossible for the nation of Israel to be cast off forever as it is to measure the heavens or to search out the foundations of the earth. God has made this fact very clear. Every time one sees the sun or the moon, there is a reminder that God has a plan and a program for Israel. That plan and program are not being fulfilled in the present age. The plan does not have its fulfillment in the nation Israel today. It is true that Israel has a political state once again in Palestine, but the nation Israel is still scattered all over the world. The Scriptures predict that there is coming a time when God will deal with the nation Israel once again.. This promise will be fulfilled in the coming millennial reign of Christ which will follow His return to the earth. The Scriptures, then, give very definitely some promises to Israel, which are not fulfilled now, but which will be fulfilled when Christ comes back and establishes His kingdom.

THE PROMISED LAND ISRAEL'S EVERLASTING POSSESSION

In the fifteenth chapter of Genesis there is a further word of God's purpose for Israel. This promise was given to Abraham concerning Israel's possession of the land. In Genesis 15:18-21 a description is given of the land God promised Israel through Abraham: "In the same day the LORD made a covenant with Abram, saying, Unto thy seed have I given this land, from the river of Egypt unto the great river, the river Euphrates." The passage continues by describing the people who live in this tremendous area of land. A further word about this is found in the seventeenth chapter of Genesis. In Genesis 17:7-8 God promises Abraham:

"And I will establish my covenant between me and thee and thy seed after thee in their generations for an everlasting covenant, to be a God unto thee, and to thy seed after thee. And I will give unto thee, and to thy seed after thee, the land wherein thou art a stranger, all the land of Canaan, for an everlasting possession; and I will be their God."

It is clear from these prophecies that God has made a very definite promise.

If one studies the geography that is back of the promise in Genesis 15, it will be found to comprehend the tremendous reach of land all the way from Egypt to the river Euphrates, which is hundreds of miles to the east. Special emphasis is given the phrase, *the land of Canaan,* in Genesis 17 where it is used in the wide sense of all the land of Palestine. Never in Israel's balmiest days did Israel possess all this land. They came close to it in the time of Solomon when much of it was put under tribute. God promised not only that He would give this land to the people of Israel, but He promised that they would possess it forever. It is perfectly obvious that the children of Israel do not possess this land today. Until they do there cannot possibly be fulfillment of the Scripture that pertains to the millennial kingdom reign of Christ.

Today Jerusalem itself is divided into two sections. Israel owns one section of it and the other section of it does not belong to Israel. Their land is divided. This again is the fulfillment of prophecy which predicted that Jerusalem would be trodden under the feet of Gentiles throughout this age. The Bible provides very definite prediction not only that Israel will continue forever as a nation, but that Israel will possess the land in its tremendous area as long as this earth continues. All of this has never been fulfilled in the past. It is not being fulfilled today. It awaits Christ's premillennial return for its fulfillment.

ISRAEL'S PROMISED KINGDOM

The Scriptures also reveal much about the character of this kingdom. In 2 Samuel 7 God gave some remarkable promises to David. David had asked about building a temple, and God had told him that his son was going to build it. In connection with this prophecy, He gave the assurance that his seed and his throne and his kingdom would continue forever. In 2 Samuel 7:16 God said to David, "Thine house and thy kingdom shall be established for ever before thee: thy throne shall be established for ever." It is quite obvious today that David is not ruling the people of Israel. There is no throne of David as far as any present fulfillment is concerned. In other words, the present age does not fulfill this promise given to David.

When Christ comes back, who is the Son of David and in the line of David as brought out clearly in the genealogy of the Gospel of Matthew, He Himself will fulfill this promise. He will reign on the throne of David over an earthly, political kingdom. He will reign not only over the house of Israel and over the land of Palestine, but we learn from other Scripture that it will extend to the entire world. But that is not true today. There is no throne of David in the earth from which Christ is reigning. If there is going to be any realistic fulfillment, it awaits the return of Christ in glory to reign over the world.

THE COMING MESSIAH

That this prophecy concerns Christ is quite clear from Isaiah 9:6-7, a great Messianic passage which Christ will fulfill:

"Unto us a child is born, unto us a son is given: and the government shall be upon his shoulder: and his name shall be called Wonderful, Counsellor, The mighty God, The everlasting Father, The Prince of Peace. Of the increase of his government and peace there shall be no end, upon the throne of David, and upon his kingdom, to order it, and to establish it with judgment and with justice from henceforth even for ever. The zeal of the LORD of hosts will perform this."

In other words, the Old Testament very directly promised that the coming Messiah would be the One who would reign upon the throne of David and fulfill the promise of a kingdom that would never end.

THE CHARACTER OF THE KINGDOM

In passing, a few Scriptures should be considered that tell what the character of this kingdom reign will be. In Isaiah 11 there is a clear picture of the reign of Christ in the kingdom. Christ will come as a rod out of the stem of Jesse. In other words, He will be a descendant of David, who is in turn the son of Jesse. In verse 2 it is declared that the Spirit of the Lord will be upon Him. In verses 3-5 the character of His reign is given: "He shall not judge after the sight of his eyes, neither reprove after the hearing of his ears: but with righteousness shall he judge the poor, and reprove with equity for the meek of the earth: and he shall smite the earth with the rod of his mouth, and with the breath of his lips shall be slay the wicked. And righteousness shall be the girdle of his loins, and faithfulness the girdle of his reins." A kingdom reign of absolute righteousness and justice is predicted.

In the present world, even in the best of countries, how much injustice and inequity there is! How many portions of the world have no real justice in our present day! When Christ comes back, there will be universal justice, the poor will be protected, the downtrodden will be cared for, and Christ Himself will reign with "a rod of iron" that speaks of absolute rule and authority, putting down every form of opposition.

Further, in this eleventh chapter of Isaiah there is a description of how the curse will be lifted. The wolf will "dwell with the lamb, and the leopard shall lie down with the kid; and the calf and the young lion and the fatling together; and a little child shall lead them." As it has often been expressed, the only way a wolf and a lamb lie down together in our present age is when the lamb is inside the wolf. But in that future age they will lie down side by side. They are not going to be enemies any more; they will be delivered from all this. There will be peace even in the natural world.

In Isaiah 11:9 the passage continues: "They shall not hurt nor destroy in all my holy mountain: for the earth shall be full of the knowledge of the Lord, as the waters cover the sea." What a contrast there is in this verse of Scripture! In our present age just a few here and there know the truth, and are really saved by faith in Christ. In that day the earth will be full of the knowledge of the Lord as the waters cover the sea. The knowledge of the Lord will be complete and abundant. Everyone will know about Christ for He will be his ruler. His glory will be manifest at the second coming in heaven. Everyone will know that Christ has returned because He is the author, the one responsible for the drastic change that will have taken place in the world order at that time.

There are many other Scriptures which could be considered. For instance, Psalm 72 pictures again how the kingdom will reach the whole world, how there will be peace and righteousness and joy, material prosperity, and all the other blessings that Christ will bring to the world for both Jew and Gentile believers of that day. Another great section is Isaiah 60—66. In the interest of brevity, however, the passages in the New Testament bearing on this subject will be considered next.

THE KINGDOM IN THE GOSPELS

It is commonly asserted that, while the Old Testament teaches that Christ will return to establish a kingdom on the earth, the New Testament contradicts this and teaches the opposite. It is contended that we must accept the New Testament's interpretation of the Old Testament. This is defined by those who advance this concept as the idea of a spiritual kingdom in which Christ reigns from heaven, such as we have in the world today. This takes the place of a literal fulfillment of these Old Testament promises, they say.

What does the New Testament teach concerning a literal kingdom of Christ on earth? Does it teach that Israel's hope is now forgotten, that there is not going to be any earthly kingdom, that the Son of David will not reign upon the throne of David?

In the first chapter of Luke the record is found concerning Mary and the announcement to her by the angel that she is to be the mother of the Messiah. This was a very dramatic pronouncement:

"Behold, thou shalt conceive in thy womb, and bring forth a son, and shalt call his name JESUS. He shall be great, and shall be called the Son of the Highest: and the Lord God shall give unto him the throne of his father David: and he shall reign over the house of Jacob for ever; and of his kingdom there shall be no end" (Luke 1:31-33).

This prediction is precisely what was revealed in the Old Testament. If anything, this promise is clearer. Here it is obvious that the Lord Jesus Christ, the Son of the Virgin Mary, will reign forever over the house of Israel. This Scripture would indicate that the New Testament confirms exactly what the Old Testament taught on this subject.

There is a further confirmation of it later. In Matthew 20:20-23 there is the record of what happened when the mother of James and John, the sons of Zebedee, came to Christ and asked that her two sons might sit upon His left hand and His right hand in His kingdom. In other words, this mother had the fond idea, when Christ reigned in the millennium, that her two sons would sit on either side of Him. Mary, the mother of James and John, was ambitious for her sons. Mothers usually think their children are wonderful and deserving of the best. Mary thought if two were to be selected, who could be more worthy than James and John? It is perfectly evident that she was looking forward to a literal fulfillment of the kingdom promises such as were given in the Old Testament. That was her understanding of it, just as it was generally of all the Jews in the first century. If there were going to be no kingdom on earth, this would be an opportune time for Christ to tell Mary so. But what does He tell her? He says to her: "To sit on my right hand, and on my left, is not mine to give, but it shall be given to them for whom it is prepared of my Father" (Matt. 20:23). It is quite clear that while the kingdom is regarded as coming, the place of honor will be given to someone else.

In Luke 22:29-30, the night before the crucifixion of Christ, He said to His disciples: "I appoint unto you a kingdom, as my Father hath appointed unto me; that ye may eat and drink at my table in my kingdom, and sit on thrones judging the twelve tribes of Israel." This dramatic statement was made, as pointed out, only the night before Christ was crucified, at the end of His earthly life. What is He teaching? He is still teaching that an earthly kingdom is coming and that the apostles will be judges of the twelve tribes of Israel in His kingdom. As one moves on through the Gospels, it is discovered that instead of contradiction we have confirmation that when Christ brings in His kingdom these things will be literally fulfilled.

CONFIRMATION OF THE KINGDOM IN ACTS

Further confirmation is found in the first chapter of Acts of the literal fulfillment of the kingdom promises. The death of Christ is already past. He has been raised from the dead and has been with His disciples some forty days. As the moment of His ascension into heaven drew near, the disciples were somewhat confused. They still did not understand much that we know with a completed New Testament. They did not comprehend that there would be a time interval between the first coming of Christ and His second coming, during which this present age should take its form and be fulfilled. They did not understand that the kingdom would follow the second coming instead of the first coming of Christ, but they still believed it was coming. And so they brought their question to Christ: "When they therefore were come together, they asked of him, saying, Lord, wilt thou at this time restore again the kingdom to Israel?" (Acts 1:6). Please note that there was no question about the kingdom being restored. The question they raised was *when* was He going to restore the kingdom to Israel? If there were not going to be any fulfillment, Christ would certainly have cleared up the whole matter by saying: "The kingdom promises will not be fulfilled. I have a different program to offer you now." But He did not say that. That was not what He had been teaching them. He had taught them that the kingdom was coming. In reply, in verse 7, "He said unto them, It is not for you to know the times or the seasons, which the Father hath put in his own power." In other words, He informs the disciples that He cannot tell them the time. It is nowhere stated in the Word of God how long this present age will be. For this reason, Christ could not tell them when the second coming would take place, and when the kingdom would follow. He told them, "It is not for you to know the times or the seasons." In other words, He was not able to give the direct answer to their question. Accordingly, in the verses which follow, He directed their thoughts to their present task. Their commission was not to bring in the kingdom or to establish the era of righteousness on earth. They were left in the world to be witnesses in what we call the interadvent period, or the period between the first and second comings of Christ. In this period they were to go forth in the power of the Spirit and to be witnesses, beginning at Jerusalem, and Judaea and Samaria, and unto the uttermost part of the world. That is our present task, too. Our responsibility is not bringing in the kingdom, but to be witnesses to the end of the earth. When Christ comes back, He will establish His kingdom and fulfill the promises.

There are many other New Testament passages which could be studied along this line; for instance, Romans 11, particularly beginning in verse 25 where there is the prediction of Israel's blindness being lifted. Israel is in blindness or hardening today, but that blindness will be lifted, Christ will come back, and the Deliverer will come out of Zion. All Israel, that is, Israel as a nation, will be delivered from their persecutors and will be brought into the place where they can enter the millennium kingdom.

CONFIRMATION OF THE KINGDOM IN REVELATION 20

The twentieth chapter of Revelation brings to conclusion the New Testament teaching on the fulfillment of the kingdom promises. The Old Testament and the New Testament consistently reveal that when Christ comes back He will reign upon the earth, but only here is the length of that reign specified. Six times in Revelation 20 the length of His reign is declared to be a thousand years. Satan will be bound a thousand years. The rest of the dead will not live again until the thousand years are finished. The wicked dead will not be raised until the end of the millennium in contrast to the resurrected saints who will reign with the Lord for a thousand years.

This chapter also makes plain that when the conclusion of the millennium comes Satan will be loosed again for a season. The judgment of God falls upon Satan at that time and those who turned to him in that climactic hour will share his fate. The present earth and the present heaven will be destroyed and a new heaven and a new earth will be created. The saints will continue in the new earth and the new heaven. The church may have its primary place in the new heaven and the Old Testament saints and Israel particularly in the new earth, though the Scriptures are not explicit on this point.

DOES THE BIBLE TEACH THAT THE PRESENT AGE IS THE PROPHESIED MILLENNIUM?

From this brief study, it is apparent that the Word of God does not teach that we are in the millennium now. Neither does it teach that the millennial reign of Christ will be brought about through preaching the gospel. Instead, it makes very evident the fact that the kingdom reign of Christ will come because of His return to this world when every eye will see Him. Everyone will be able to see His glory, and know His power. The knowledge of the Lord will reach over the whole world and His government will be from sea to sea. In the Scriptures there is the constant reminder that the hope for this world in all its chaotic condition today, and with all its hopelessness from a moral standpoint, is the coming of the Lord. Our expectation is that Christ will come back, and that He will deal with this world in judgment, destroying the wicked and establishing the righteous in His kingdom on the earth.

THE IMPORTANCE OF THE PREMILLENNIAL RETURN OF CHRIST

At the beginning of this study the question was raised: What difference does it make whether we believe in the premillennial return of Christ or not? Obviously, only one of the three millennial views that were presented can be right. Each of the views has a different interpretation of a large body of Scripture and a different concept of the present age. Determining which view is right is very important as we study the Word of God because it concerns so many Scriptures as well as so many practical reasons.

Only the premillennial viewpoint makes any real sense of the whole Word of God. The great prophecies given in Scripture concerning Israel, Gentiles, and righteousness and peace on the earth will never be understood unless they are linked with the teaching of the premillennial return of Christ. There are some very practical reasons, however, why this is important.

Only the premillennial return of Christ and the teachings associated with it provide a literal interpretation of Scripture. In other words, if one is free to explain away everything in Scripture by spiritualization if it does not agree with his particular theory, then it is not important what theory is followed.

But if one is trying to interpret the Bible literally, trying to take it just the way it is written and to believe what it says, he will be led to a firm belief in the premillennial return of Christ.

There are other reasons why it is very important. The teaching of the Scripture which gives the premillennial return of Christ its proper emphasis is the only viewpoint which shows Israel in its right place. The amillennial view usually contends that there is no further prophecy to be fulfilled concerning Israel. And the postmillennial view sets forth much the same argument. In other words, it is only the premillennial doctrine that gives Israel its right to the fulfillment of its promises in the Word of God.

There are also additional reasons why the premillennial view is important. It was held by the early church. The early church fathers were confessedly those who held to the premillennial return of Christ. In fact, for the most part only heretics opposed premillennialism until Augustine, late in the fourth century and hundreds of years after the apostles. The early church believed Christ would come back to earth before the millennium. While the details of their doctrine are not always clear, the impartial view of most scholars who have studied what the early fathers have written is that they held the premillennial hope of Christ's return and the millennium to follow.

There is yet another reason why premillennialsm is important. There is no greater bulwark against modern liberalism than the doctrine of the premillennial return of Christ. A postmillenarian can be almost anything as far as other beliefs are concerned. He can be a conservative, a modernist, or in between. The same is true of an amillenarian. He might be a liberal, a Roman Catholic, a Greek Catholic, or a conservative Protestant. An intelligent premillenarian, however, is usually straight on other doctrine. He believes the Bible to be the Word of God. He believes in the deity of Christ and is orthodox in other respects. Modernists are never premillenarians. One of the best ways of fortifying the laity against the inroads of modernism in our day is to teach them premillennial truth. If they hold this doctrine, they will not be tempted to go off into false doctrines. If they understand what the Word of God teaches, they will not be led to embrace various isms and cults. While some false cults have propagated a form of premillennialism, their teaching concerning premillennial doctrine is quite removed from the historic interpretation.

The premillennial return of Christ is not an insignificant matter, but is a very important doctrine. It is the key that unlocks the great treasures of the prophetic word; it sets everything in its right perspective, and gives an intelligent understanding of the reason we are in a chaotic state today. It reveals from the Word of God how He will bring righteousness to this wicked world.

Many who believe in the premillennial return of Christ also hold that He is coming for His church and that this coming for His church is an event which will precede even the premillennial return. This event also will occur before the beginning of the predicted time of the tribulation. That Christ could come today is our imminent hope. This is our message, our expectation, our answer to a world that is dark with gloom. We have the blessed hope of Christ's return for the church and His later premillennial return to establish His kingdom on the earth.

THE COMING JUDGMENT

If these truths are faithfully taught as found in the Word of God, they serve to remind us that a day is coming when

God will deal in judgment with this world. In that day the most important question any heart can face is the question of whether he has trusted this Person who alone can set this world right, who in His first coming died on the cross and provided salvation for all who would trust in Him, and in His second coming will establish righteousness and peace on the earth.

Are you trusting in this wonderful Savior? He is presented as the only hope for the world but, more important, He is the only hope for you. If we are trusting Him as our personal Savior, we know that when these great climactic events take place we will be on the Lord's side. We will share His righteous reign over the earth as the bride of Christ, and our place will be a blessed estate for all eternity.

Chapter IV

THE IMMINENT TRANSLATION
OF THE CHURCH

The Hope of the Early Church

EVER SINCE the Lord Jesus was taken from His disciples to glory on the day of His ascension, the hope of His imminent return has been the constant expectation of each generation of Christians. In the early church this was a dominant theme of the apostles' teaching and an impelling motive in their witness. As gradually the great truths about the purpose of God in the church were unfolded and the present age began to extend, the hope of His return continued undimmed. At the close of the last book of the New Testament, the aged Apostle John still breathes a prayer, "Even so, come, Lord Jesus" (Rev. 22:20).

Unbelief and Confusion on This Doctrine Today

The passing centuries have brought scoffers who have said, "Where is the promise of his coming?" (2 Pet. 3:4). It is the fashion of our day in high theological circles to discount the doctrine of the coming of the Lord and to isolate this portion of Scriptural teaching as outside the realm of scholarly investigation. We are told that Paul and the other apostles were mistaken and naive to hope for the coming of the Lord in their day. Others, while admitting the teaching of the Scriptures on this doctrine, have interposed various prophesied events and thereby have postponed the hope of His return by generations and even millenniums. Resulting controversies have obscured and confused the blessed hope of the imminent return of the Lord Jesus Christ.

THREE LEADING QUESTIONS

Before an intelligent understanding of the issues involved in the hope of the imminent return of the Lord can be achieved, three main questions must be considered: (1) Can we believe the Bible and accept its revelation literally? (2) Are there predicted events which must occur before the Lord's return? (3) Do the Scriptures present the fulfillment of the hope of His return as an imminent event, i.e., as possible of fulfillment at any moment?

For the purpose of the present study, in answer to the first question, we must assume the inspiration of the Scripture and the validity and infallibility of its revelation. The present chaotic condition in prophetic study has come partly through failure to accept the Bible as the Word of God.

The answer to the second question is one of the most complicated in the whole field of prophecy. Many schemes of interpretation have been offered. The postmillennial view interposes a whole millennium between the present and the coming of Christ, thereby postponing that glad event by at least a thousand years. The posttribulationists believe the church must continue on earth through the Day of the Lord, including that unprecedented and indescribable time of trouble on the earth culminating in the great tribulation which Christ predicted (Matt. 24:21) and of which the Apostle John gives great detail (Rev. 6—19). If either of these two views—the postmillennial or the posttribulational—is correct we must give up the doctrine of the imminent coming of the Lord and must look instead for either a millennium on earth or a time of great tribulation.

WHAT DO THE SCRIPTURES TEACH?

The Bible teaches, according to the premillennial interpretation, both the doctrine of a millennial kingdom of righteousness on earth and the awful time of tribulation which will precede it. The question is whether Christ will come first, before both of these predicted periods, to meet His church in the air and take her home to glory. This we believe to be the teaching of the Scripture and the only view which fully resolves all the problems of interpretation involved.

THE WORD OF COMFORT TO THE THESSALONIANS

In 1 Thessalonians 4:13—5:11, the great truth of the coming of the Lord is expounded. One can gather from this section that Paul had taught the Thessalonians much of this doctrine in his brief stay with them (Acts 17:1-10), but some questions remained. One of these questions concerned those of their number who had already passed into the presence of the Lord. *When* would they be raised from the dead? That they would be raised no one doubted, but would they be raised at the time the Lord came for the living saints or would it be later? This is answered emphatically in this passage. The dead in Christ would be raised first, just a moment before the living saints were caught up to meet Christ in the air. On the basis of this hope, they were exhorted, "Wherefore comfort one another with these words" (1 Thess. 4:18). The word which is translated *comfort* in both the Authorized and Revised Standard Versions includes the idea of *exhort* and *encourage*. This was to be a great encouragement and comfort to them—their reunion with their loved ones was no more distant than their reunion with the Lord when He came for His own.

Having established the *order* of the resurrection and translation, the next question was the *time*. When was the event to occur? In chapter five this is answered. Under the term "day of the Lord" (1 Thess. 5:2) the period immediately following the translation is described. It will come as a thief in the night—unexpected by those in that period (1 Thess. 5:2). It will involve "sudden destruction" and "they shall not escape" (1 Thess. 5:3). In contrast to these overtaken so suddenly by destruction, this trouble will not overtake the saints (1 Thess. 5:4). The reason is that the saints are "children of light" and "children of the day" (1 Thess. 5:5). "For God hath not appointed us to wrath, but to obtain salvation by our Lord Jesus Christ" (1 Thess. 5:9; cf. Rev. 6:17). In a word, the contrast is made sharply between those translated and those left on earth so unexpectedly to destruction while the church is caught up to be with the Lord. The day of wrath, destruction, and judgment will *follow* the translation. The church will not be included in the wrath poured out upon the earth (1 Thess. 5:9). The teaching of the apostle in this passage establishes not only the order of resurrection and translation but also the relation of these events to the time of tribulation which follows.

The very exhortation of comfort of the Lord's return loses its meaning if the church must pass through the great tribulation. What comfort can there be to a prospect of distant deliverance if in the path between there is probably martyrdom, destruction, and persecution? Far better to die a normal death and be raised in the resurrection than to endure such a period in order to avoid death in translation. The whole point of the Thessalonian passage hangs on the imminency and pretribulational character of the coming of the Lord.

THE WORD OF REVELATION TO THE CORINTHIANS

The fifteenth chapter of 1 Corinthians is rightly known as

the resurrection chapter. With its gospel introduction (1 Cor. 15:1-4) it first argues the resurrection of Christ as an essential of Christian faith and hope, and then links this with the resurrection of men in general. Having established these great truths, in the close of the chapter, by sharp contrast, the grand exception to the doctrine of resurrection is revealed: "Behold, I shew you a mystery; We shall not all sleep, but we shall all be changed, in a moment, in the twinkling of an eye, at the last trump: for the trumpet shall sound, and the dead shall be raised incorruptible, and we shall be changed" (1 Cor. 15:51-52).

This passage is obviously parallel to 1 Thessalonians 4. It is the time of the resurrection of the dead and translation of the saints. The subject is introduced as a "mystery." As used in the New Testament, this word refers to truth "hid" from Old Testament revelation, but now revealed in the New. That there should be a resurrection of the just is certainly no mystery. Nor is it a mystery that there should be living saints on the earth at the time of that event. Both of these general factors are clearly indicated in the Old Testament (cf. Dan. 12:2; Zech. 12:10). The mystery is that the living saints shall be translated, "changed" from a mortal body to an immortal body "in a moment, in the twinkling of an eye, at the last trump" (1 Cor. 15:52). This is nowhere taught in the Old Testament. It should be carefully noted that this transformation is for "all"— "not all sleep, but we shall all be changed" (1 Cor. 15:51).

This teaching demands a time interval between the event here revealed and the coming of the Lord to establish His kingdom on earth. In other words, this event must occur *before* the tribulation while the kingdom is established by the coming of the Lord to the earth *after* the tribulation. The necessity of this conclusion is plainly implied in the passage before us. According to the premillennial interpretation of Scripture, during the millennium there will be tilling of the ground, raising of crops; there will be marriage, increase in population, and death. Amos speaks of the plowman, planting, the vineyards, the making of gardens, and eating of their fruit (Amos 9:13-15). That this refers to the millennium is made clear because the promise is related to the final gathering from which there will be no more plucking up out of the land (Amos 9:15). If this is true, there must be a body of saints still in the flesh, not resurrected, and not translated, to perform these natural functions. Further, this body must be on the earth at the time of the Lord's coming to establish His kingdom on earth. But, according to the 1 Corinthian passage, *all* the living saints at the time of the Lord's coming for the church are translated, leaving no redeemed to fulfill a natural function on earth. The only way both concepts can be fulfilled is for a time interval—the seven years anticipated in Daniel 9:27—to elapse between the translation of the saints of this age and the return of Christ to establish His kingdom. In this period a new generation of believers can be formed. In other words, the passage in 1 Corinthians is left without an adequate interpretation unless Christ comes for His own before the tribulation.

Posttribulationists have no explanation of this problem and usually choose to ignore it. The truth is that the great Scriptures of the Old and New Testaments dealing with the return of the Lord to establish His kingdom at the end of the tribulation *never* speak of a translation at that time. The saints on earth who greet Christ on that occasion remain on the earth, in the flesh, and enter the millennial kingdom as either redeemed Gentiles or redeemed Israel. By contrast, the redeemed of this present age are translated, changed, and caught up to glory.

In view of this tremendous revelation, the apostle concludes the section: "Therefore, my beloved brethren, be ye stedfast, unmoveable, always abounding in the work of the Lord, forasmuch as ye know that your labour is not in vain in the Lord" (1 Cor. 15:58). Our hope is translation, not resurrection; the coming of the Lord, not the tribulation.

Let Not Your Hearts Be Troubled

Probably the first recorded revelation clearly distinguishing the translation of the saints from the establishment of the kingdom on earth after the tribulation is found in John 14 in the tender context of the Upper Room Discourse. Peter had just been informed that he would deny his Lord thrice. All were troubled at the Lord's words, "Whither I go, ye cannot come" (John 13:33). Then came the comforting exhortation, "Let not your heart be troubled" (John 14:1). They are exhorted to believe in God and also to believe in Him. Simply the Lord unfolds the tremendous revelation: "In my Father's house are many mansions: if it were not so, I would have told you. I go to prepare a place for you. And if I go and prepare a place for you, I will come again, and receive you unto myself; that where I am, there ye may be also" (John 14:2-3). Here is the explanation of the reason why they could not follow Him now and why He was going to leave them. He was coming back to take them to the prepared place in the Father's house. What a contrast this is to the Jewish expectation understood by the disciples! The Jews were looking for an earthly kingdom promised by the prophets. Christ was expected to rule on the throne of David on earth. But this was different. Christ says here that He would take His own to heaven, to the Father's house. This was to be their expectation as believers in this present age. With this they were to comfort their hearts and for this they were to wait.

In the light of the later revelation given in Thessalonians

and Corinthians, it should be evident that we have in John 14 a parallel passage. Christ is speaking of the time of the translation of the saints. Obviously, the disciples could not go to the Father's house apart from such a transformation of body and spirit. The important fact was that the Lord was coming for them and the time of separation, however long, was only temporary.

In Thessalonians it was revealed that the translated and resurrected saints would meet the Lord in the air. In John we learn where they go from that meeting place. They go to heaven, to the Father's house. The place has been prepared by the loving Bridegroom for His bride. How fitting to leave behind the world with its cares and sins and to be taken into the glorious presence of the Father's house! Those who believe the church will go through the tribulation think otherwise, however. For them the meeting in the air is just a momentary event followed by immediate return to the earth with the Lord to establish His kingdom and to destroy His enemies. The church corporately, for them, never goes to heaven at all. If they are right, the place prepared in the Father's house will never be used by the resurrected and translated church. Instead, the church will be plunged immediately into the millennial earth and afterwards into the newly created new heaven and new earth. How much better the interpretation that gives full luster to the hope of the imminent return of Christ as an event before the time of tribulation with its provision for the refuge in heaven while the storms of divine wrath purge the earth and fit it for the millennial state! Such a hope brings solace to hearts wounded by separation and longing for the face of the Beloved. There is no cloud between, no wearisome events of ominous proportions standing between us and that glad moment. In the twinkling of an eye the transcending event is accomplished and the church is forever with the Lord.

Every Man That Hath This Hope

The truth of the Lord's coming was intended to be a comfort, an exhortation, and a hope that quiets troubled hearts. In 1 John we have a further truth as a counterpart to that revealed in the Gospel:

> "Beloved, now are we the sons of God, and it doth not yet appear what we shall be: but we know that, when he shall appear, we shall be like him; for we shall see him as he is. And every man that hath this hope in him purifieth himself, even as he is pure" (1 John 3:2-3).

What a prospect! We shall be like Him when we see Him. This is not a reward for long toil and walking the weary road. This is the love token of a Bridegroom to the bride. The transformation, of which Paul wrote in 1 Corinthians 15, is to transfigure the bride until she, like the Bridegroom, is altogether lovely and without a trace of sin or disfigurement. This is not merely a sentiment, an ecstasy of anticipation. This is a purifying hope. "Every man that hath this hope in him purifieth himself, even as he is pure."

As in the other passages considered, the imminency of the Lord's coming is that which underlines and emphasizes the meaning of the exhortation. It is because it is a moment-by-moment expectation that the believer is exhorted to holiness. It is as if a distinguished guest were expected at any moment. Everything must be in order and spotless. There will be no time for preparation when he comes. Not only is there the customary cleaning; but as the moments of waiting continue there is the constant reinspection to be assured that all is in order. If it were known that the guest would not arrive for days or months or years, there would be no need of vigilance. It is the *imminency* of his coming that determines the urgency for preparation.

So it is with the coming of the Lord. Many there are for whom this hope is dim and distant. By reason of theology or unbelief, they are assured that there is yet plenty of time for preparation. Much must intervene first before the Guest comes, they believe. For such His coming is not a purifying hope. But, "Every man that hath this hope in him purifieth himself, even as he is pure." Those who really believe in the imminent coming of the Lord are more mindful of their purity than of anything else, more eager to see His face than to participate in things of the earth. So may it be with us. May the coming of the Lord be a blessed hope, a purifying hope, a comforting hope, a steadfast hope, the ray of light in a dark world, the path to glory!

Chapter V

THE SEVENTIETH WEEK OF DANIEL

THE INTERPRETATION of the revelation given to Daniel concerning the seventy weeks (Dan. 9:24-27) constitutes one of the determining factors in the whole system of prophecy. The attention given to it by all schools of interpretation, and the attacks upon the authenticity of the book itself combine to focus the white light of investigation upon it. The interpretation of this passage inevitably colors all other prophetic views, and a proper understanding of it is the *sine qua non* of any student of prophecy.

The Importance of The Revelation

The importance of the revelation of Daniel 9 lies first of all in the chronology which it establishes. The major outline is given of the period from Daniel to Christ and from the rapture of the church to the second coming of Christ in glory. Certainly, no other Old Testament passage does as much for ordering events future from Daniel's point of view as does the passage under consideration.

Properly interpreted, the prophecy of Daniel furnishes an excellent example of the principle that prophecy is subject to literal interpretation. Practically all expositors, however opposed to prophecy *per se,* agree that at least part of the seventy weeks of Daniel is to be interpreted literally. In fact, the force of the literal interpretation is such that those who deny the possibility of accurate prophecy are compelled to move the date of the

writing of Daniel until after the events which they believe fulfilled it. If the first sixty-nine weeks of Daniel were subject
to literal fulfillment, it is a powerful argument that the final
seventieth week will have a similar fulfillment.

Another important aspect of the passage is frequently overlooked by expositors. The seventy weeks of Daniel, properly
interpreted, demonstrate the distinct place of the Christian church
and Israel in the purposes of God. The seventy weeks of Daniel
are totally in reference to Israel and her relation to Gentile
powers and the rejection of Israel's Messiah. The peculiar purpose of God in calling out a people from every nation to form
the church and the program of the present age are nowhere
in view in this prophecy.

THE HISTORIC FULFILLMENT OF THE SIXTY-NINE WEEKS

The interpretation of the seventy weeks of Daniel is divided
into two main problems, the fulfillment of the sixty-nine weeks,
and the fulfillment of the seventieth week. Our present study
is primarily concerned with the latter problem. However, in
order to have a background for judgment and interpretation,
it is necessary to survey briefly the various interpretations of the
first sixty-nine weeks.

There are few passages of Scripture which have occasioned
a greater variety of interpretations than Daniel 9:24-27. A comparison of commentaries reveals that seldom can two be found
with exactly the same exegesis. As James A. Montgomery states
in concluding his long discussion of the passage:

> "To sum up: The history of the exegesis of the 70 Weeks
> is the Dismal Swamp of O. T. criticism. The difficulties that
> beset any 'rationalistic' treatment of the figures are great
> enough, for the critics on this side of the fence do not agree
> among themselves; but the trackless wilderness of assump-
> tions and theories in the efforts to obtain an exact chronology

fitting into the history of Salvation, after these 2,000 years
of infinitely varied interpretations, would seem to preclude
any use of the 70 Weeks for the determination of a definite
prophetic chronology."[1]

While we do not share Montgomery's pessimism, there is a be-
wildering lack of unanimity among expositors.

Most of the difficulty of expositors in the study of this
passage may be traced to their premises. In general, there are
two main divisions of interpretation: Christological and non-
Christological. The former interprets the first sixty-nine weeks
of Daniel as culminating in Christ while the latter finds fulfillment of Daniel's prophecy in events before or after Christ.
Most writers on the subject have not been slow to notice the
repeated use of the number *seventy* in relation to the prophetic
program. It had been predicted that Israel's servitude under the
Babylonians would last seventy years. The seventy years were
inflicted because of her failure to observe her Sabbatic years
(Lev. 26:34-35; 2 Chron. 36:21). The plan for the Sabbatic years
involved the basic number *seven*. Sir Robert Anderson also ad-
vances the interesting conclusion that it was exactly 490 luni-
solar years (360 days each) or seventy times seven years from
the dedication of the temple in the eleventh year of Solomon
to the dedication of the second temple in 515 B.C.[2] These facts
have led expositors to seek a literal fulfillment of Daniel 9:24-27.

The non-Christological interpretation of the passage attempts
to find fulfillment of the seventy weeks in the events leading
up to the persecution of Antiochus IV, known commonly as
Antiochus Epiphanes. In 168 B.C., a pagan altar was constructed
on top of the great altar of burnt sacrifices, and a pagan sacri-

---

[1] *International Critical Commentary: Daniel,* pp. 400-1.
[2] *The Coming Prince,* p. 71, note.

fice was offered under the rulership of Antiochus Epiphanes.[3] The act precipitated the Maccabean revolt which Antiochus attempted unsuccessfully to put down with great cruelty .(167-164 B.C.). The system of chronology adopted by those who interpret Daniel to prophesy this event varies with the writer.

Generally, there is agreement among them that the seventy weeks of Daniel began with the beginning of the seventy years of Jeremiah. The beginning of the servitude of Jerusalem in 606 B.C. does not, however, give a satisfactory terminus for the first seven weeks, or forty-nine years of the prophecy. Accordingly, Montgomery quotes with approval the view that the seventy weeks began at 586 B.C., when Jerusalem was completely desolated according to his chronology and the forty-nine years accordingly bring us approximately to 538 B.C. when the Jews were permitted to return to Jerusalem. The sixty-two weeks or 434 years begin at 538 B.C. and culminate in the desecration of Antiochus in 168. As is apparent, however, there are two drastic errors in this system of computation. The beginning of the seventy weeks did not begin with the Jeremiahic prophecy but with the command to restore Jerusalem, which is identified most satisfactorily as occurring in 445 B.C. The terminus of the seventy weeks does not take us to 168 B.C as would be expected, but to 104 B.C. There is an error, here, of more than sixty years which no amount of juggling can erase.

Montgomery solves the problem by conveniently determining that Daniel was in error in his calculation:

> "To be sure, a similar objection may be made against our identification of the final Week of the Seventy with the period of Ant.'s tyranny, for the 62 Weeks would then take us down some 65 years too far. We can meet this

[3]*International Standard Bible Encyclopaedia, s.v.,* "Abomination of Desolation."

objection by surmising a chronological miscalculation on the part of the writer [Daniel]. For the first 49 years he had exact Scriptural information; he was profoundly conscious of the epochal character of his own age; there was the necessity of extending Jer.'s 70 years into a much larger figure in order to bring it up to date (the natural process of all interpretation of prophecy), and the 70 years became 70 Year-Weeks, 490 years, too high a figure indeed, but he was not embarrassed, in the absence of a known chronology, in squeezing these 434 years between the Return and the Antiochian persecution."[4]

It will be noticed that the interpretation of Daniel's seventy weeks to make them fulfilled in the Antiochian persecution involves the premises: (1) Jeremiah was wrong; (2) Daniel was in error; (3) the Christological view is not worthy of serious consideration even though it provides for a literal interpretation. For anyone having a serious view of the inspiration of the Scriptures, this non-Christological interpretation must be dismissed as being only a clumsy attempt to counter the better interpretations which provide for a literal fulfillment. It is really no solution at all.

A more interesting non-Christological view is advanced by the Jews themselves. The prevailing interpretation of the Jews after A.D. 70 was that the events of Daniel's seventieth week have their fulfillment in the destruction of Jerusalem. Like other forms of the non-Christological view, they are not too concerned with a literal fulfillment of Daniel's chronology, though their interpretation is more satisfactory than the view of the destructive higher critics. Some aspects of their interpretation find their way even into the Christological view as portrayed by some writers.

The Christological view, which finds the sixty-nine weeks

─────────────

[4]Montgomery, op. cit., p. 393.

of Daniel culminating in Christ, has been accepted by most conservative expositors. The Fathers from the second to the fourth century abound in explanations which bring the culmination of the sixty-nine weeks to the period of Christ's public ministry and death.[5] The most satisfactory solution of the Christological interpretation is that of Sir Robert Anderson, a view that fully honors the accuracy and authority of Daniel's revelation.[6] His conclusions embrace the following points: (1) the seventy weeks of Daniel represent 490 years, divided into three parts: forty-nine years, four hundred and thirty-four years (following the first forty-nine years), and the last week of seven years. (2) There was only one decree ever issued for the rebuilding of Jerusalem—that given to Nehemiah and its date is 445 B.C., specifically the first of Nisan or March 14 of that year. (3) The city was actually rebuilt during the time of Nehemiah at the end of the prophesied desolations of Jerusalem. (4) The sixty-two weeks, or 434 years, immediately follow the first forty-nine years, and on the basis of a prophetic year of 360 days total 173,880 days, which would end April 6, A.D. 32— the probable date when Christ rode into Jerusalem in fulfillment of Zechariah 9:9.

The chronology of Sir Robert Anderson has a number of distinct advantages over other systems. It provides a literal fulfillment of the prophecy of Daniel. It is based on sound historical and chronological data. Most of all, it presents an interpretation of Scripture which fully honors the doctrine of inspiration. If a system of interpretation based on carefully established principles can bring the fulfillment of the prophecy into such accurate detail, it is ridiculous to attempt to warp Daniel's prophecy into some sort of interpretation which admittedly does not

[5] *Ibid.*, pp. 398-99.
[6] Sir Robert Anderson, *op. cit.*

fulfill the chronology of the passage. If Antiochus missed the proper date by more than sixty years, by occurring too soon, and the destruction of Jerusalem obviously occurred too late, undoubtedly all true scholars would immediately embrace the Christological interpretation if it were not for prejudice either against the person of Christ, as in the case of the Jew, or against a literal fulfillment of prophecy, as in the case of the destructive critics. The case for the Christological interpretation, particularly the viewpoint of Sir Robert Anderson, stands on every point superior to other views.

The important point of the Christological interpretation is that the first sixty-nine weeks had a *literal* fulfillment, both as to details and as to chronology. In approaching the task of interpreting the prophecy concerning the seventieth week, we must, in all fairness to the principles approved by the fulfillment of the sixty-nine weeks, expect a literal fulfillment of the seventieth week both in its detail and in its chronology. The beginning of the seventy weeks of Daniel was marked by a definite event. At the end of the sixty-nine weeks, or 483 years, there was a definite break in the prophecy which was fulfilled literally by the death of Christ. Likewise, the final week of the prophecy, the seventieth week, apparently has a definite beginning and ends with the "full end" of the period of desolations. There are indications in the text that a considerable time period elapses between the close of the sixty-ninth week and the beginning of the seventieth week. The question naturally arises, and it is decisive: Is the seventieth week of Daniel future, or has it been fulfilled already in history? To this question we now direct our thought.

HAVE THE EVENTS OF DANIEL'S SEVENTIETH WEEK BEEN FULFILLED?

There are at least five theories in regard to the fulfillment

of the prophecy concerning the seventieth week of Daniel; that
is, most interpretations can be classified in one of five categories. Those who find the fulfillment of the first sixty-nine weeks
in the events of the Maccabean persecution usually find the fulfillment of the seventieth week in the same period of persecution. As this view·has been previously found to fail in fulfill-
ing the passage, their interpretation of the fulfillment of the
seventieth week likewise fails. The view of the Jews that the
seventieth week is fulfilled in the events surrounding the destruction of Jerusalem in A.D. 70 likewise fails in fitting the chronology of Daniel.

Three other views have commended themselves to conservative scholars. There are some who hold that the seventieth
week of Daniel is an indefinite period beginning while Christ
was on earth and extending to the consummation of all things.
This is in harmony with Daniel 9:24, which indicates that the
program of God for bringing in everlasting righteousness and
cessation of Israel's persecutions will be completed by the end
of the seventieth week. This interpretation breaks down completely, however, as a literal fulfillment. The chronology of the
sixty-nine weeks established the principle of literal fulfillment,
and we cannot for the sake of convenience postulate an indefinite period for the final week of the prophecy. While we cannot
accept this spiritual interpretation of the passage, it is an interesting confession on the part of those who accept it that *history
does not record events which correspond with the prophecy of
the seventieth week.*

One other view, however, claims our serious attention. It is
advanced by a number of able expositors and claims to be a
literal interpretation. In brief, the view accepts a system of
chronology which allows for the termination of the sixty-nine
weeks of the prophecy at the baptism of Christ. The first half

of the seventieth week is, in their judgment, fulfilled by the events of the public ministry of Christ. In the middle of the week Christ is crucified, the sacrifice and oblation cease, and the events of the last half of the seventieth week are immediately fulfilled in the events which follow. The seventy weeks terminate, perhaps, in some event such as the conversion of Cornelius. In other words, the seventieth week has already been fulfilled literally, and we cannot look for any future fulfillment.

In opposition to this view, the interpretation is advanced that there is an indefinite period of time between the close of the sixty-ninth week and the beginning of the seventieth week. At some future date the seventieth week will begin, and its events will come to pass literally and will follow the chronology of the seven years of the seventieth week of Daniel. This is the only view which provides a reasonable ground for believing the final week of Daniel is future. If we accept the premise that the final week of Daniel demands a literal fulfillment, we are shut up to the last two views named: that it was fulfilled literally in the first century before A.D. 40, or that it is future and we can look for a literal fulfillment at some future date. The two explanations oppose each other; both cannot be right. Accordingly, we may well weigh the contentions of those who support each view as a basis for decision.

One of the cleverest writers to support the interpretation that the seventieth week of Daniel is already fulfilled is Philip Mauro, whose views are set forth in his volume, *The Seventy Weeks and the Great Tribulation.* Mauro believes that God's purpose for Israel as a nation was finished upon their rejection of Christ and that the promises given to Israel are now being fulfilled in the church. He denies the possibility of a future millennium to fulfill the promises of a kingdom given to David and Israel. His work is accordingly prejudiced by his premises;

but his appeal is to the Scriptures rather than human authority and for this reason his contentions should be weighed. He states the case in support of his position with all the force of an astute thinker and skillful debater. It is characteristic of his style, however, that he never discusses facts for which he does not have a ready solution; i.e., he selects for discussion only those points which are in favor of his viewpoint. This defect is too often overlooked by the unwary. He also has great skill in magnifying a minor point until it appears to be a decisive one, at the same time passing rapidly over material which might upset his argument. Accordingly, it is more important to consider what he does not say, on some points, than what he states.

Philip Mauro's system of interpretation, in brief, involves the following points: (1) The first sixty-nine weeks of Daniel run from the decree of Cyrus (536 B.C.) to the baptism of Christ. As this period totals 562 years rather than 483, Mauro, while insisting on literal fulfillment, claims that there can be no certainty of the exact historic length of years between the decree of Cyrus and the baptism of Christ—in fact, he claims to find an error of eighty years which adjusts the difference.[7] (2) The baptism of Jesus is the fulfillment of the prophecy, "to anoint the most holy" (Dan. 9:24), the anointment being the descent of the Holy Spirit, and the "most holy" being Christ Himself. (3) The "prince that shall come" is Titus, and the one who makes the covenant of Daniel 9:27 is Christ. (4) The cessation of the sacrifices in the middle of the seventieth week is the fulfillment of Old Testament sacrifices by the death of Christ. (5) All the six elements of the decree in relation to "thy people" and "thy holy city" mentioned in Daniel 9:'24 are fulfilled by the life, death, and resurrection of Christ. (6) There cannot be any break between the sixty-ninth and the seventieth week of

---

[7] Philip Mauro, *The Seventy Weeks and the Great Tribulation*, pp. 23-25.

Daniel: "Never has a specified number of time-units, making up a desired stretch of time, been taken to mean anything but *continuous* or *consecutive* time-units."[8]

The issue between the two literal interpretations of Daniel's seventieth week is, then, clearly drawn. A glance at the six points enumerated will readily reveal that some of them are decisive in the interpretation. All six elements of the decree relating to Israel and Jerusalem must be fulfilled by the death of Christ. If so much as one of these was not fulfilled, then the interpretation is revealed to be faulty. If the one who makes the covenant is *not* Christ, it is admitted even by Mauro that the seventieth week must be still future: "Manifestly those two ideas stand or fall together; for if verse 27 relates to Christ, then the last week followed immediately after the 69th; but if it relates to antichrist, or a coming Roman prince, then it is yet future."[9] If the sacrifices actually ceased at the death of Christ, it would do much to substantiate Mauro's contention. While the final point—i.e., that there cannot be a break between the sixty-ninth and seventieth weeks—is begging the question, it is well to consider what parallels the Scripture may afford on the question.

Is Titus the prince that shall come? According to Daniel 9:26, *after* the sixty-ninth week (sixty-two and the first seven weeks) the "anointed one" shall be "cut off," and "the people of the prince that shall come shall destroy the city and the sanctuary." It is clear that the "anointed one" is Christ—the Authorized translation is correct, "Messiah." But who are "the people" and "the prince"? It is a well-established fact of history that Jerusalem was destroyed in A.D. 70 by the Roman armies, to the utter destruction of upwards of one million Jews in the area. The people represented here can be none other

---

[8]*Ibid.*, p. 95.
[9]*Ibid.*, p. 94.

than those of Rome. The "prince of the people" is accordingly a Roman prince. The interpretation of Mauro is that this is clearly the character Titus who led the armies of Rome in A.D. 70 against Jerusalem. There are good reasons, however, for believing that the character thus introduced is to be identified with the future political ruler of the Mediterranean world in the time just before the second coming of Christ. Mauro flatly denies that there will be any such ruler, denies that the Roman people of the first century are to be identified in any way with the people of that future time.

It is not necessary to engage in a disputation of Mauro's entire system to show his error in this particular. It is a plain fact of history that God is dealing with the Jews of today in a way determined by the rejection of Christ by their fathers. If this can be true, then why should it be thought incredible that a future prince should be identified as Roman and as connected with the people who destroyed Jerusalem? Mauro overlooks a most significant fact in his chronology, however. If Titus is the "prince" of Daniel 9:26, then the destruction of Jerusalem occurred after the seventieth week, rather than after the sixty-ninth week. Is it not utterly inexplicable that the prophecy of verse 26 should be stated to be *after* the sixty-ninth week, if in matter of fact it is during and after the seventieth week? Does not the way in which the truth is stated imply that the events occur *after* the sixty-ninth week *before* the seventieth week? If so, a parenthesis is called for, allowing for all events in their proper place and for a fulfillment of the seventieth week in the future.

Not only does the form of the prophecy imply a parenthesis between the sixty-ninth and seventieth weeks, but the expression, "the people of the prince," is unusual. Normally, it would be expected that the prophecy would state that the prince would destroy the city. In Daniel 7 and 8 are found prophecies dealing with military triumphs and they are spoken of as being consummated by their leader. In Daniel 9:26, however, the usual form of statement is turned around and it is stated that "the people of the prince" destroyed the city. Now, it is clear that such would be the case if the prince had no direct connection with the event, but Jerusalem was destroyed under the personal direction of Titus. The language of the prophecy would seem to indicate that some other person than Titus was in view.

The Scriptures of the Old and New Testament contribute prophecies concerning the coming of a military leader who will rule the Mediterranean world. From Revelation 13:1-10, we gather that he will be the greatest military ruler in power that the world has ever seen. A comparison of Revelation 13 with the events of the destruction of Jerusalem reveals no similarity and must refer to a future event. Other passages (Dan. 7:8, 11, 24-27; 11:36-45; 2 Thess. 2:1-12) apparently refer to the same person. In view of the revelation of Daniel 7, it is not strange to find another reference in Daniel 9.

Who makes the covenant for one week? Mauro strenuously objects to identifying the "prince that shall come" with a future political ruler, not so much because it contradicts the plain meaning of verse 26 but because it provides an interpretation of verse 27 which utterly destroys his theory. In verse 27 it is revealed: "And he shall make a firm covenant with many for one week: and in the midst of the week he shall cause the sacrifice and the oblation to cease; and upon the wing of abominations shall come one that maketh desolate; and even unto the full end, and that determined, shall wrath be poured out upon the desolate." It is normal exegesis for a pronoun to claim as its antecedent the nearest noun with which it could be identified. The nearest antecedent in this case is the "prince that shall come."

This could not be Titus for he did not make such a covenant, and according to Mauro's theory the seventieth week must immediately follow the sixty-ninth—and Titus did not appear on the scene until years later. Accordingly Mauro identifies the one who makes the covenant as Christ.

In support of Mauro's contention is the fact widely recognized by the Scriptures and expositors of the Scripture that Christ is the minister of the new covenant and that in His death on the cross the new covenant was duly executed. An attempt to connect Daniel's covenant with the new covenant, however, is a work of desperation rather than a natural exegesis. The new covenant is expressly called an "everlasting covenant" (Heb. 13:20). The covenant of Daniel 9:27 continues only for one week in its intent, and if the break at the middle of the week may be so interpreted, the covenant is broken before it runs its course, i.e., at the end of the first half of the week. The two covenants have nothing in common as to their duration.

It is also widely accepted that the new covenant was enacted by the death of Christ. Mauro's theory would require that the death of Christ occur at the beginning of the seventieth week. Because of the fact that he believes the death of Christ occurred in the middle of the week, he is forced to the conclusion that the covenant is made *in* the week rather than *for* one week—in opposition to the usual translation. It is obvious that Mauro's interpretation requires an unnatural exegesis.

A fact of great significance is that the covenant is made with "the many" which could only refer to "thy people" (Dan. 9:24), Israel. The new covenant, in so far as it relates to Israel, is connected in Scripture with their millennial blessings and the future regathering of Israel (cf. Heb. 8:8-12). Mauro, however, flatly denies that Israel has any place in God's future program. He believes that the covenant mentioned in Daniel

9:27 is a covenant of grace toward all people as contained in the present gospel of grace. Mauro, accordingly, is faced by a dilemma. If this is indeed a covenant between Christ and Israel regarding their future blessing, then his whole system breaks down for the passage would teach a future for Israel as such. The alternative is to admit that the covenant is not the new covenant and that Christ is not the one who enters into the covenant. Mauro's escape from this dilemma is to deny what the passage plainly teaches—that the seventy weeks refer specifically to "thy people," Israel, and "thy city," Jerusalem. In the last analysis, there is nothing whatever in the revelation concerning this covenant (Dan. 9:27) to connect it with Christ.

Were Old Testament sacrifices ended by the death of Christ? The argument concerning the identity of the one who makes the covenant is decisive in itself. If Christ did not make the covenant, then the last of the seventy weeks is yet awaiting fulfillment. A further question, however, has an important bearing on the issue. According to Daniel 9:27, the sacrifice and oblation are stopped in the midst of the seventieth week by the one who makes the covenant. According to Mauro, this is the event of the death of Christ which supplanted Old Testament sacrifices. Mauro quotes from Hebrews 10:8-9, where it is stated: "He taketh away the first, that he may establish the second." Mauro asks: "What perfect agreement with the words of the prophecy, 'He shall cause the sacrifice and oblation to cease'!"[10]

This is an important point. If indeed the death of Christ causes the sacrifice and oblation to cease, it would be a powerful argument in support of Mauro's view. That the new covenant supplants the old and the one sacrifice of Christ supplants the many sacrifices of the old covenant is indeed the teaching of the Scriptures. It is something else, however, to state that He

---
[10]*Ibid.*, p. 85.

caused the sacrifice and oblation to cease. As a matter of fact, *the sacrifice and oblation did not cease until the temple was destroyed in* A.D. 70. It was the ruthless work of violence of the Roman armies that cause the sacrifice and oblation to cease in the first century, and, if we interpret the passage correctly, the seventieth week of Daniel is a prophecy of a future restoration of these sacrifices under a covenant and their violent conclusion. Even the Epistle to the Hebrews speaks of the fact that at the time of the writing of the epistle, probably shortly before the destruction of Jerusalem, the priests were still ministering in the temple—more than thirty years after the death of Christ. In Hebrews 8:4 we read: "Now if he were on earth, he would not be a priest at all, seeing there are those who offer the gifts according to the law" (A.S.V.). The argument is that Christ is a priest in heaven, not on earth, as there are still priests on earth serving according to the law of Moses. The Scriptures themselves are careful, then, by using the present tense, *are,* to include evidence which makes Mauro's interpretation inadmissible.

Have the desolations of Daniel's seventieth week been fulfilled? Mauro is probably more embarrassed by the lack of a good explanation of the latter part of Daniel 9:27 than by any other feature of his interpretation. His system requires that the seventieth week of Daniel be a definite time period of seven years. It is therefore necessary that the desolations of the latter part of verse 27 be fulfilled within a period of three and one-half years of the death of Christ—according to his system. Mauro comes to the conclusion, however, that the desolations in this verse are those accomplished by the armies of Titus in A.D. 70. In other words, Mauro is unable to find any event within the seventieth week of Daniel to fulfill the prophecy of the latter part of Daniel's seventieth week, and in the end is forced to abandon his major thesis that the prophecies of Daniel's seventy weeks are subject to literal fulfillment.

In contrast to Mauro's difficulty, we have in Matthew 24:15, from Christ Himself, the prophecy of the fulfillment of Daniel's promised desolations. Christ said: "When therefore ye see the abomination of desolation, which was spoken of through Daniel the prophet, standing in the holy place (let him that readeth understand) . . ." The context which follows indicates that the events are preliminary to the second coming of Christ. In fact, so direct is the connection that some who, like Mauro, connect Matthew 24:15 with the destruction of Jerusalem under Titus have attempted to find fulfillment of the promise of Christ's return in the events of A.D. 70. Instead of the desolations of Daniel 9:27 being fulfilled in connection with the destruction of Jerusalem, they are rather one of the signs pointing to the early return of Christ in glory.

The declared purpose of God for the seventy weeks. One of the decisive questions facing any interpreter of Daniel 9:24-27 is the question whether God's declared purpose for that period has been fulfilled. In that period, according to Daniel 9:24, it is God's purpose to (1) finish transgressions, (2) make an end of sins, (3) make reconciliation for iniquity, (4) bring in everlasting righteousness, (5) seal up vision and prophecy, (6) anoint the most holy. It is Mauro's interpretation that points one through four were fulfilled by the death of Christ; point five is the resulting spiritual blindness which befalls Israel; point six is fulfilled by the anointing of the church on the Day of Pentecost.

There are many interesting details involved in the discussion of each of these points which in the interest of brevity we cannot consider. It is of great importance to gain a clear view of the principles which dominate the interpretation, however.

Mauro *must* find fulfillment of all the purpose of God revealed here before the end of the period extending three and one-half years beyond the death of Christ. In his interpretation, he claims to find such fulfillment, and it is this claim we now examine.

There are many details in his system which are open to question. For instance, he claims fulfillment of the prophecy that vision and prophecy are "sealed up," by which he means that Israel comes into *permanent* spiritual blindness. He perhaps overlooks the fact that God used Jews to write the New Testament after the date he claims for the close of Daniel's seventieth weeks—Jews without an exception if Luke was an Israelite. While Paul reveals that blindness in part befell Israel because of their rejection of Christ, it is also clear that the blindness will be lifted after the fullness of the Gentiles is come in (Rom. 11:25). Mauro's interpretation of the anointing of the most holy, that it refers to the baptism of Christ, while supported by some, is in violation of the consistent usage of the Old Testament. Tregelles states on this point, "The expression does not in a single case apply to any *person*."[11] It is a better interpretation that it refers to a future return of the Shekinah glory. The American Standard Version margin renders it, "a most holy place."

All these details are significant, however, before the principal objection to Mauro's interpretation. According to the specific limitation of Daniel 9:24, the prophecy pertains to "thy people," Israel, and to "thy city," Jerusalem. To make it plain, then, transgressions must be finished *in relation to Israel and Jerusalem;* and end must be made to sins, and iniquity must *be purged away* (cf. A. S. V. margin) *in relation to Israel and Jerusalem;* everlasting righteousness must be brought in *for Israel and Jerusalem;* and so on through the prophecy.

---

[11]Tregelles, *Daniel*, p. 98, as cited by Anderson, *op. cit.*, p. 51.

What does Mauro do with the passage? For him the passage deals with the whole world, a general provision of salvation through the death of Christ which, according to his interpretation, does not relate to Jerusalem or to Israel as such at all. Jerusalem is scheduled only for destruction and Israel to be utterly cast off—according to Mauro's view. To make this prophecy of coming blessing to Israel and Jerusalem—which can be fulfilled only by the return of Christ to bring in a kingdom of righteousness—a reference to the work of Christ on the cross is to confuse the work of God in Christ on the cross and its application historically. The benefits of the death of Christ will be realized by Israel only after "they shall look unto me whom they have pierced; and they shall mourn for him . . ." (Zech. 12:10), and in the day when "a fountain" be "opened to the house of David and to the inhabitants of Jerusalem" (Zech. 13:1)—events still future from our point in history. Sir Robert Anderson has demonstrated that none of the prophecies of Daniel 9:24 have been fulfilled: "A careful study of the Angel's words will show not so much as one of them has been thus accomplished."[12]

Is a parenthesis between Daniel's sixty-ninth and seventieth week unparalleled in Scripture? The entire burden of Mauro's argument is intended to support his contention that there is no break between the sixty-ninth and seventieth week of Daniel. He not only holds that the passage does not admit such an interpretation; but he states that such an interpretation would be a violation of a consistent principle in Scripture that time units are *always* continuous. To quote his exact words: "Never has a specified number of time-units, making a described stretch of time, been taken to mean anything but *continuous* or *consecutive* time units."[13]

---

[12]*Op. cit.*, p. 79.
[13]*Op. cit.*, p. 95.

Fortunately, for the brevity of our own study here, there is an entirely adequate answer to this statement. Not only does the internal evidence of the passage demand it by stating certain events are *after* the sixty-ninth week rather than in or after the seventieth week, but there are parallel cases in the Scripture where God, as it were, stopped the clock of fulfillment only to resume the progress of fulfillment later.

The monograph of H. A. Ironside, *The Great Parenthesis,* is a worthy and timely contribution to the subject. Ironside shows a number of instances of parentheses in God's program: (1) The interval between the "acceptable year of the Lord" and the "day of vengeance of our God" (Isa. 61:2)—a parenthesis already extending more than nineteen hundred years. (2) The interval between the Roman Empire as symbolized by the legs of iron of the great image of Daniel 2 and the feet of ten toes (cf. also Dan. 7:23-27; 8:24-25). ' (3) The same interval is found between Daniel 11:35 and 11:36. (4) A great parenthesis occurs between Hosea 3:4 and verse 5, and again between Hosea 5:15 and 6:1. (5) A great parenthesis occurs also between Psalm 22:22 and 22:23 and between Psalm 110:1 and 110:2. (6) Peter, in quoting Psalm 34:12-16, stops in the middle of a verse to distinguish God's present work and His future dealing with sin (1 Pet. 3:10-12).

(7) The great prophecy of Matthew 24 becomes intelligible only if the present age be considered a parenthesis between Daniel 9:26 and 9:27. (8) Acts 15:13-21 indicates that the apostles fully understood that during the present age the Old Testament prophecies would not be fulfilled, but would have fulfillment "after this" when God "will build again the tabernacle of David" (Acts 15:16). (9) Israel's yearly schedule of feasts showed a wide separation between the feasts prefiguring the death and resurrection of Christ and Pentecost, and the feasts

speaking of Israel's regathering and blessing. (10) Romans 9—11 definitely provide for the parenthesis, particularly the figure of the olive tree in chapter 11. (11) The revelation of the church as one body requires a parenthesis between God's past dealings and His future dealings with the nation Israel. (12) The consummation of the present parenthesis is of such a nature that it resumes the interrupted events of Daniel's last week.

To this imposing list of arguments for the parenthesis between Daniel's sixty-ninth and seventieth week, we can add the interesting computations of Sir Robert Anderson in regard to the statement in 1 Kings 6:1, that Solomon began to build the temple in the 480th year after the children of Israel were come out of Egypt. A computation of the evidence indicates that this period was, instead, 573 years.[14] On the basis of a study of Judges, Sir Robert Anderson discovered a total of 93 years during which Israel was cast off as a nation—divided into five different periods of time (cf. Judges 3:8, 14; 4:2-3; 6:1; 13:1). By subtracting this from 573, the figure is corrected to 480, the exact figure stated by the writer of 1 Kings.

CONCLUSION

The answer to our leading question—Is the seventieth week of Daniel future?—can only be given in the affirmative. The Scriptures bear a full testimony that God has a purpose yet unfulfilled for His people, Israel. If the events of Daniel's seventieth week are future, it is clear that the person who makes the covenant must be the wicked character who is the persecutor of all who will not worship him. The "many" with whom the covenant is made can be, on the basis of the context, only Israel, still in unbelief. The "end" of which Daniel 9:27 speaks can be only the return of Christ to bring righteousness, peace,

[14]Anderson, op. cit., pp. 81 ff.

prosperity, and universal knowledge of the Lord to this evil world. Before the world will witness these stirring events, we who are His look for that blessed moment when, caught up from this world at the return of the Lord for His own, we shall see His face and forever thereafter know one passion and one love—to worship and serve our blessed Lord.

Chapter VI

WILL THE CHURCH GO THROUGH
THE TRIBULATION?

THOUSANDS of Bible-believing Christians believe that the coming of the Lord for His church is imminent; that is, it could happen any day, any moment. They believe when this event takes place that Christians will be translated, receiving instantly glorious bodies suited for life in heaven. At the same moment, the dead in Christ will be raised from their graves and with those translated will be caught up to meet the Lord in the air. Thus will begin an eternity of bliss in the presence of the Lord.

The hope of the imminent return of the Lord is as old as the church. The apostles anticipated the coming of Christ that could occur at any time. Early in his ministry, Paul exhorted the Thessalonians "to wait for his Son from heaven" (1 Thess. 1:10). They were told to "comfort one another with these words" (2 Thess. 4:18) when their loved ones fell asleep in Jesus. Later Paul wrote Titus that Christians should be "looking for that blessed hope, and the glorious appearing of the great God and our Saviour Jesus Christ" (Titus 2:13). The Apostle John records late in the first century the words of Christ to the disciples the night before He was crucified: "I will come again, and receive you unto myself; that where I am, there ye may be also" (John 14:3).

The early church fathers understood the Scriptures to teach that the coming of the Lord could occur any hour. To quote one authority, in the Didache (about A.D. 120) Christians were exhorted: "Watch for your life's sake. Let not your lamps be quenched, nor your loins unloosed; but be ye ready, for ye know not the hour in which our Lord cometh" (cf. *Ante-Nicene Fathers,* VII, 382). In the "Constitutions of the Holy Apostles" (Book VII, Sec. ii, xxxi) a similar quotation is found: "Observe all things that are commanded you by the Lord. Be watchful for your life. 'Let your loins be girded about, and your lights burning, and ye like unto men who wait for their Lord, when He will come, at even, or in the morning, or at cock-crowing, or at midnight. For what hour they think not, the Lord will come; and if they open to Him, blessed are those servants, because they were found watching' . . ."(cf. *Ante-Nicene Fathers,* VII, 471). It should be clear to any impartial observer that the early church believed in the imminent coming of the Lord, but without solving many problems related to it.

The church soon became involved in problems other than the study of prophecy, however, and church councils in the fourth century and in following centuries were concerned primarily with the doctrine of the Trinity, the doctrine of sin, and various controversies. Paganism and ritualism engulfed the church after the fourth century, and it was not until the Protestant Reformation in the sixteenth century that Biblical doctrines began to be restored. In the period since the Protestant Reformation, attention has again been directed to prophecy. More concentrated study has been directed toward prophetic interpretation in the last hundred years than any similar period in church history.

Further study of prophecy, particularly among premillenarians, has raised some problems that had not been considered before. One of the major problems is that specific signs are given in Scripture for the coming of Christ to establish His righteous kingdom on earth as predicted by the Old Testament prophets and confirmed in the New Testament. A great period of unprecedented tribulation is described, for instance, by Christ (Matt. 24:15-26). The general period of tribulation is revealed to be seven years—a conclusion reached from Daniel's seventieth week, equivalent to seven years (Dan. 9:27). The last half of this period is the great tribulation. The Book of Revelation devotes many chapters to the same event. Obviously, if this period of trouble must precede the coming of Christ to establish His kingdom, how then can His coming be a daily expectation?

If the coming of Christ for believers in this age is imminent, it must occur before these predicted signs and before the tribulation period. Hence, many have come to believe that the coming of Christ for His church is an event which takes place *before* the tribulation time while the coming of Christ to establish the kingdom on earth occurs *after* the tribulation. In confirmation of this conclusion, students of the prophetic Word find abundant proof to sustain these conclusions. While as many as twenty-five arguments could be advanced in support of the translation of the church before the tribulation, for the sake of this brief discussion seven principal reasons will be presented.

THE DOCTRINE OF IMMINENCY

It is commonly recognized today by serious Bible students that if the coming of Christ is after the tribulation, then His coming cannot be imminent. Too many events are pictured as preceding His coming to allow it to be a daily expectation if He does not come for His church until after the tribulation. Exhortations to the church to "wait" and to "look" for His appearing are hard to explain if signs must be fulfilled first. We should be looking for the signs instead. The blessed hope of an imminent return would be separated from us, then, by the awful period of tribulation. To many it is a precious hope to be looking daily for the Lord. This is also one of the practical reasons why thoughtful Christians believe this doctrine is important and worth defending.

THE DOCTRINE OF GOD'S PURPOSE FOR THE CHURCH

Many careful Bible students distinguish the purpose of God for Israel and God's purpose for believers in this present age. God is now supremely revealing His grace in the salvation of Jew and Gentile alike. Believers since Pentecost are regarded as the body and bride of Christ, a company distinct from Israel's program and promises. With the beginning of the tribulation period, however, if premillenarians are right, God will resume His program for Israel in preparation for His millennial reign upon the earth.

It seems most logical to believe that His program for the present age will be finished before God resumes His announced program for Israel in the tribulation. In confirmation of this, there is no reference to the church as the body and bride of Christ in any of the tribulation passages. Believers in the tribulation are referred to only by general terms such as *saints* and the *elect*—terms used for believers all through the Bible. Thus in Revelation, chapters 4—19, describing the tribulation, there is no mention of the church as a body of believers. By contrast, Revelation, chapters 2—3, mentions the church many times.

THE DOCTRINE OF THE TRIBULATION

The tribulation itself is of such character as to raise serious question whether the church will be required to pass through it. Those who deny the translation of the church before the tribulation usually also deny that it is going to be as terrifying as the Scriptures describe it, and make it equivalent to troubles and trials common to life now. In the Scriptures, the tribulation is described as a definite period of trouble unprecedented in all history. Daniel describes it as "a time of trouble, such as never was since there was a nation . . ." (Dan. 12:1). Christ spoke of it as "great tribulation, such as was not since the beginning of the world to this time, no, nor ever shall be" (Matt. 24:21). The Book of Revelation describes it as an outpouring of the wrath of God upon an unbelieving world (cf. Rev. 6:17), a time when apostasy and sin reach unprecedented blasphemy. It is a period which brings death to most of the earth's population and destruction to civilization. Nothing like it has ever happened before. It seems out of keeping with the present age of grace to inflict on the last generation of believers such a series of catastrophes. In fact, there are definite promises that point to deliverance before the day of wrath comes.

SPECIFIC PROMISES

In John 14:1-3, in connection with the promise of Christ, "I will come again," the purpose of His coming is revealed to be to take believers to "my Father's house," by which term He describes heaven. After He meets the church in the air, He will take them to the place prepared. In contrast, at His coming to establish the millennial kingdom, all believers remain in the earthly scene. In 1 Thessalonians 5:4-10, believers are assured that they are children of light, not children of darkness. They are comforted with the promise that the day of wrath will not overtake them as a thief, as it will the world. They are promised, "For God hath not appointed us to wrath, but to obtain salvation by our Lord Jesus Christ" (1 Thess. 5:9). In 1 Thessalonians 1:10 our hope is stated: "To wait for his Son from heaven, whom he raised from the dead, even Jesus, which delivered us from the wrath to come." If believers are delivered "from the wrath to come," why inflict upon them a day of wrath designed for the ungodly? Are not believers assured: "Much more then, being now justified by his blood, we shall be saved from wrath through him" (Rom. 5:9)? In Revelation 3:10 the godly church at Philadelphia is promised: "Because thou hast kept the word of my patience, I also will keep thee from the hour of temptation, which shall come upon all the world, to try them that dwell upon the earth." In a word, they are promised that they will be kept "from" the period of tribulation ahead. That is different from being kept "through" this time.

This promise was true for the historic church at Philadelphia because they had the hope of the Lord's return before the tribulation. If this church prefigures the true church as a whole, as many believe, it points to a further conclusion that all true believers in this age will have the same hope. This seems to follow a pattern found even in the Old Testament. Noah was saved from the flood. He was borne safely above it. Lot was led out of Sodom before its destruction. Rahab was saved before Jericho fell. Enoch was translated before the flood. While analogies are not conclusive, the translation of the church before the tribulation would be in keeping with these precedents.

REMOVAL OF THE HOLY SPIRIT

According to 2 Thessalonians 2:3-12, the one now restraining sin in the world will be removed from earth's scenes before the beginning of the Day of the Lord, which includes the day of wrath. While there has been much discussion as to the identity of the restrainer, the best answer is that it refers to God's restraining hand, more specifically to the work of the Holy Spirit resisting the rising tide of sin in the world. It is clear that this restraint is removed during the tribulation time. Obviously, the Holy Spirit cannot be taken away while resident in the church in the world as is now the case. A chronology can thus be set up— the church indwelt by the Holy Spirit removed from the earth; then, the man of sin is revealed; with his appearance the tribulation begins. While the Holy Spirit continues to be omnipresent, His work will be similar to the period before Pentecost, but with His restraint withheld.

NECESSITY OF AN INTERVAL BETWEEN THE TRANSLATION AND THE ESTABLISHMENT OF THE MILLENNIAL KINGDOM

A number of events which seem to occur after the translation of the church and before the establishment of the millennial kingdom requires an interval of some years duration. According to John 14:1-3, the believers in this age go to heaven when Christ comes. There they will be judged for rewards (2 Cor. 5:10). There, too, the marriage will take place between the church as the bride and the Lord as the bridgegroom (Eph. 5:25-27). After His coming, they are forever together—"Where I am, there ye may be also" (John 14:3). Again, "so shall we ever be with the Lord" (1 Thess. 4:17).

It is clear from Scripture that there will be a believing remnant on the earth when Christ comes back to establish His millennial kingdom. This remnant is never identified with the church and is never spoken of as translated. It is composed of believing Jews and Gentiles living at the close of the tribulation (Ezek. 20:34-38; Matt. 25:31-46). After the second coming, they are still in the flesh and are not free from death. They till the ground, raise crops, bear children, and repopulate the earth (Isa. 65:20-23; 66:20-24; Zech. 8:5; Matt. 25:31-40). Not a single passage in the Old or New Testament related to the Lord's coming to establish His kingdom ever speaks of a translation of living believers. It should be obvious why this is true. If the translation of all believers took place at the end of the tribulation, there would be none left to fulfill these prophecies of a godly remnant still in the flesh to populate the millennial earth. Evidently, the church after the Lord's coming is not going to raise crops in the earth, bear children, repopulate the earth, and be subject to death. An interval of time is demanded, then, during which another generation of believers will come into existence. While every believer will be translated when Christ comes for His church, a new body of believers will be formed in the awful days of the tribulation. Those of this group who escape martyrdom will be the believing godly remnant on the earth when the Lord returns with His church from heaven to establish His millennial kingdom. In view of these facts, it is impossible to make the translation of the church and the establishment of the millennial kingdom simultaneous.

CONTRASTS BETWEEN THE TRANSLATION AND THE COMING TO ESTABLISH THE KINGDOM

These can be stated as (a) translation; (b) coming to establish His kingdom:

(a) Translation of all believers;	(b) no translation at all.
(a) Translated saints go to heaven	(b) translated saints return to the earth.
(a) Earth not judged;	(b) earth judged and righteousness established.
(a) Imminent;	(b) follows definite predicted signs including the tribulation.
(a) Not in the Old Testament;	(b) predicted often in the Old Testament.

(a) Believers only;	(b) affects all men.
(a) Before the day of wrath;	(b) concluding the day of wrath.
(a) No reference to Satan;	(b) Satan bound.

These contrasts should make it evident that the translation of the church is an event quite different in character and time from the return of the Lord to establish His kingdom, and confirms the conclusion that the translation takes place before the tribulation.

CONCLUSION

While earnest Christians differ on the question, many Bible students who have specialized in the field of prophecy believe that the Scriptures teach a pretribulation translation of the church. A striking evidence for this is found in the manifestos issued by the International Congress on Prophecy in meetings held in 1942, 1943, and 1952, in Calvary Baptist Church, New York City. In each of these international congresses, about thirty outstanding prophetic teachers took part. In each congress a manifesto was issued setting forth their convictions regarding prophetic truth. All three congresses went on record in favor of the translation of the church before the tribulation without so much as a dissenting vote. The representative character of these congresses is illustrated by the fact that ten of the thirty-one speakers at the 1952 congress were presidents of evangelical schools—colleges, Bible institutes, and seminaries—whose orthodoxy sets a standard for evangelicalism. Many different denominations were represented. In spite of diverse backgrounds, the expressed unanimity reflects the mature conclusions reached by these leaders in prophetic study.

Before the first coming of the Lord, there was confusion

even among the prophets concerning the distinction between the first and second comings (1 Pet. 1:10-11). At the present time, there is similar confusion between the translation of the church and the second coming to establish the millennial kingdom. An attitude of Christian tolerance is called for toward those who differ on this doctrine. But may we all "love his appearing" (2 Tim. 4:8).

Chapter VII

IS ISRAEL CAST OFF FOREVER?

A LMOST EVERY aspect of the predicted future for Israel constitutes a decisive factor in the structure of prophetic interpretation. The construction that is placed upon passages in Scripture dealing with the future of Israel inevitably determines the whole scope of prophecy. One of the obvious facts which all systems must face is that Israel is just as surely in the New Testament as in the Old, and the phenomena of the preservation of Israel as a distinct people through centuries of dispersion have called for some adequate explanation.

Among those who take Scripture seriously, two attitudes have emerged. Some have denied any future to Israel, attempting to find all of Israel's future included in the Christian church; i.e., whatever future is assigned to them is identical with that of Gentile believers. Others have held that there is a future day of blessing for Israel as a distinct people. The former view is held by those who follow an amillennial interpretation of prophecy, while the latter view is held by those who hold the postmillennial and premillennial systems of interpretation. With the current disrepute of postmillennialism, it has remained for the premillennial and amillennial systems to uphold their respective interpretations. The issue is rather clearly defined, though too often the premises assumed settle the argument before it begins. It is the thesis of this discussion that the amillennial viewpoint involves a distortion of numerous passages of Scripture and an oversimplification of prophecy which is not warranted by the prophetic Word. The issue of Israel's future should be settled by investigation into the plain statement of Scripture regarding it. To this end, the present discussion deals with a crucial and important doctrine, viz., the subject of Israel's spiritual blindness and whether or not Israel is cast off forever. It is predicted in Scripture that the present blindness of Israel will in the future be removed and that certain important results will follow. The nature and importance of this doctrine will be evident in its effect on Israel's future.

FOUR INTERPRETATIONS

The key passage to the doctrine of Israel's blindness or "hardening" is found in Romans 11:26: "For I would not, brethren, that ye should be ignorant of this mystery, lest ye should be wise in your own conceits; that blindness in part is happened to Israel, until the fulness of the Gentiles be come in." The passage seems to reveal that a blindness or hardening has befallen Israel at the present time, that this blindness will terminate at the time designated as the "fulness of the Gentiles." The verse following which constitutes a part of the same sentence goes on: "And so all Israel shall be saved: as it is written, There shall come out of Sion the Deliverer, and shall turn away ungodliness from Jacob." In other words, there seems to be a definite time sequence: first, Israel is blind, then Israel's blindness is ended and "all Israel shall be saved." The passage calls for specific events which involve the whole scheme of prophecy. Does Israel have a future? Is there a day coming of spiritual blessing for Israel? When will "all Israel" be saved?

In an attempt to answer these leading questions, at least four interpretations of the passage have arisen. Origen, the father of the allegorical method of interpretation, seems to be the originator of the idea that the passage teaches only the general truth that there will be opposition and blindness in relation to the gospel which will be gradually overcome, resulting in the end in "all Israel"—meaning, according to Origen, all believers—being saved. This interpretation, of course, robs the passage of any specific meaning and does violence to its terms.

The attitude of the Reformers was only a slight improvement over Origen. Encouraged perhaps by the prominence given this verse by the ardent millenarians of that day, they denied that the passage taught any general future conversion of Israel, affirming that it merely taught that the hardened and blind condition of Israel did not prevent some from entering the church. The prejudice against allowing any foothold for the millenarians is illustrated in Calvin's deliberate mistranslation of the "until" as "that," and by Luther's famous statement to the effect that the Jews are the devil's children and impossible to convert (*zu bekehren ist unmoglich*). Calvin, like Origen, makes "all Israel" equivalent to the "whole people of God"; i.e., the church. The effect of both views is to deny Israel any literal fulfillment of their prophetic future and to consider them cut off forever as a people.

The third type of interpretation is typical of nineteenth-century postmillennialism, and Charles Hodge may be taken as an example. Holding, as does any consistent postmillennial system, that there is going to be a fulfillment of the prophecies relative to an earthly kingdom of peace and righteousness on the earth, the exponents of this view find the fulfillment of the many promises related to Israel in this period. Charles Hodge, accordingly, interpreted Romans 11:25 as predicting "a great and general conversion of the Jewish people, which should take place when the fulness of the Gentiles had been brought in, and that then, and not till then, those prophecies should be fully accomplished which speak of the salvation of Israel."[1] He goes

---

[1] Charles Hodge, *Epistle to the Romans*, p. 584.

on to write that this view has been the position of every age of
the church except the period of the Reformers. He lists eight
formal arguments in support of this interpretation.

The fourth interpretation is typical of twentieth century
premillennialism. It holds with the postmillennial viewpoint
that Israel has a future, but it insists that this future is more
than a mere spiritual revival. The future of Israel is a restoration of Israel as a nation as well as a people, and it involves the
fulfillment of a literal kingdom on earth with Christ as King.
The present age is one of Gentile blessing; the future age will
be one of Israel's blessing. The two periods are just as distinct
as that of Israel before Pentecost and the present age. It is a new
dispensation in which the place of Gentiles and Israel in privilege
and blessing is reversed. Now is the time of the fullness of Gentile
blessing and privilege. The future day will place Israel first.

The problem of interpretation raised in this discussion is
solved by proper exegesis of Romans 11:25 in its context. It
may be observed before turning to this, however, that the viewpoint of Origen or of Luther is no solution to the problem at
all. The allegorical system of interpretation, of which Origen is
the father, is theological quicksand for this doctrine as for all
others. If the Scriptures are to be subject to a fanciful interpretation according to the whims of the interpreter, it is obvious
that no solution to any problem can be found for the simple
reason that the very existence of the problem is denied. Problems
arise from an attempt to arrive at the plain and literal meaning
of the Scriptures. The viewpoint of the Reformers in regard
to Israel is also unsatisfactory and provides no solution to the
problem of interpretation. Their attitude was evidently prejudiced and their interpretation is governed by opinion rather than
exegesis. In the heat of the controversies of the Reformers, the
millennial issue was cast aside rather than weighed, and the

future of Israel in Scripture suffered the same fate. The doctrinal problem of Israel's future must be solved by an appeal to the written Word and an attempt to find its revelation on this important theme.

WHAT HAS BEFALLEN ISRAEL?

It is the plain teaching of Romans 11:25 that something has happened to Israel. What occurred is described as a "blindness" (King James Version) or "hardening" (American Standard Version). The Greek word *porosis* refers to *"the covering with a callus"* (Thayer). In the other two instances in which it occurs in the New Testament (Mark 3:5; Eph. 4:18), it is used in reference to "hardening of the heart." The absence in Romans 11:25 of the qualifying phrase, "of the heart," left the translators in a dilemma and occasioned the various translations: "blindness" or dulling of the sight, and "hardening" or dulling of the senses more generally. According to A. T. Robertson, the word is used by Hippocrates as a medical term, and means in the New Testament "obtuseness of intellectual discernment, mental dulness."[2] From the word itself, then, it is clear that the affliction befalling Israel has to do with their reception of God's message and revelation. In respect to this, they are blind or hardened. What is the nature of this blindness?

It is the position of most commentators who deal with this problem that the blindness of Israel had a long history before Christ. It is not difficult to trace the lack of understanding on the part of Israel of God's revelation and purposes throughout the entire Old Testament period. Certainly in the time of Moses, during the Judges, and the periods of the early and latter prophets, Israel manifested a dullness of spiritual understanding of which Isaiah complained. Paul refers to this frequently by

[2]A. T. Robertson, *Word Pictures in the New Testament*, IV, 398.

reference to Moses, David, and Isaiah in Romans 10 and 11. It is also clear that the whole human race, without distinction between Israel and Gentiles, are spiritually blind by virtue of their depravity and cannot see apart from a work of God in enabling grace. In what sense has something befallen Israel which is unusual and distinct?

The key to the problem is afforded by the use of the word *mystery*. The doctrine of Romans 11:25 is referred to as a "mystery." By this word reference is made to a doctrine which had not been received prior to the New Testament revelation, but which is now fully made known—as Robertson puts it, "the revealed will of God now made known to all."[3] In whatever sense, then, Israel was blind before Christ, a new Judgment of God has fallen upon them after rejecting Christ. Whereas the former blindness had to do with the *prophetic* revelation, the latter blindness had to do with the *fulfillment* in Christ. Israel, which of all nations should have recognized the credentials of Christ, leads the Gentiles in being slow of hearing and understanding. By designating Israel's blindness as a mystery, a new aspect is therefore added.

It is also included in the revelation that this blindness is "in part." The expression "in part" quite clearly refers to the fact that the blindness is not universal. The veil is lifted for some at least, and individual Jews like Paul have believed in Christ. The thought is not that all Israel is partially blinded. While the majority of Israel are usually and distinctively blinded, a few are granted as exceptions and this occasions the "in part." Whether or not Martin Luther could have been persuaded that he was wrong in denying that the Epistle to the Romans teaches that Jews can be converted, it is rather apparent that this is the

---

[3]*Ibid.*, IV, 397.

teaching of the passage. The situation of blindness in part is the abiding condition of Israel in this age.

WHAT IS THE MEANING OF "UNTIL"?

The central teaching of the passage revolves on the preposition *until*. The condition of Israel's blindness is revealed to continue up to a certain point at which it is terminated. That this expression is crucial to the interpretation is borne out by the attempts to alter its force. Calvin, for instance, changes it to "that," making the blindness of Israel a factor in bringing about the fullness of the Gentiles. This is a violation of the meaning of the expression. As Charles Hodge states, "The words . . . cannot, so consistently with usage, be translated, *as long as,* or *so that,* followed as they are here by the aorist subjective; see Rev. xv. 8, xvii. 17; compare Heb. iii. 13."[4] A. T. Robertson follows the same translation, labeling the clause a "temporal clause" meaning "until which time."[5] Its basic meaning is "up to."[6] In the language of Thayer, it indicates "the terminus ad quem." If we are willing to accept the plain meaning of the Greek text, we must recognize that this passage teaches two distinct situations: (1) one in which Israel is blinded in part; (2) another in which this blindness is removed. This is what the passage states and any tampering with it is confession of prejudice.

WHEN WILL ISRAEL'S BLINDNESS BE ENDED?

The exegesis of Romans 11:25 has indicated a predicted time when Israel's blindness will be ended. This time is described as the point in the prophetic program when "the fulness of the Gentiles be come in." This expression, which occurs only here

---

[4]Charles Hodge, *op. cit.,* pp. 586-87.
[5]*Op. cit.,* IV, 398.
[6]A. T. Robertson, *A Grammar of the Greek New Testament in the Light of Historical Research,* Fifth Edition, p. 639.

in the New Testament, has given rise to many interpretations. Charles Feinberg summarizes the various viewpoints as follows: "Sanday and Headlam maintain that *to pleroma* refers to the Gentile world as a whole. Griffith Thomas refers the time to the close of the Gentile dispensation. Faber, Stifler, Brookes, and Chalmers are all of the opinion that the time referred to is identical with 'the times of the Gentiles.' Godet, after denoting the fulness of the Gentiles as the totality of the Gentile nations, designates the time as 'the times of the Gentiles.' Bosworth contends that reference is made to the large majority of the Gentile population of the world, while Govett thinks the phrase refers to the elect of this dispensation out of all nations. Moule holds that *eiselthe* ('be come in') refers to a time when the ingathering of the Gentile children of God will be not at an end, but running high."[7] There is obviously much difference of opinion on the subject.

It is not necessary to the argument that Romans 11:25 predicts a future time of blessing for Israel to settle with finality the meaning of the expression, "fulness of the Gentiles." It clarifies the situation, however, to arrive at some understanding of the meaning of the term. While the Scriptures do not explicitly expound the term, it is evidently the antithesis of the "fulness" of Israel mentioned in Romans 11:12: "Now if the fall of them [Israel] be the riches of the world, and the diminishing of them the riches of the Gentiles; how much more their [Israel's] fulness?" The present age is the time of the fall of Israel and the riches of the Gentiles. The passage clearly implies that in a future period the fullness of Israel will come and that in it the Gentiles will have even more blessing that at present. The meaning of the passage is, then, simply that the Gentiles will have their full time of blessing and that this will be followed

---

[7]Charles L. Feinberg, "The Mystery of Israel's Blindness," unpublished thesis filed in the Dallas Theological Seminary Library, pp. 69-70.

by Israel's time of blessing. The "until" of Romans 11:25 would mark the close of the Gentile period as such.

Within the bounds of the premillennial interpretation of Scripture, a problem remains regarding the termination of the period of Gentile blessing. In Luke 21:24 Christ referred to the "times of the Gentiles" as continuing as long as Jerusalem is "trodden down of the Gentiles." The reference in Luke is to the political domination of Jerusalem by Gentiles, which began with the fall of Jerusalem at the time of the captivity and has continued to the present day. While the terminology is not significant in itself, from the context of the two passages involved it seems clear that the expression "times of the Gentiles" has reference to political domination of Gentiles, while the expression "fulness of the Gentiles" has reference to Gentile blessing and opportunity in this present age. If this analysis is correct, the times of the Gentiles and the fullness of the Gentiles are two entirely different ideas. The times of the Gentiles began long before Christ and will continue until Christ returns to establish His kingdom. The fullness of the Gentiles began at Pentecost and will continue only as long as the present age of grace lasts. From the standpoint of prophecy, the important point is that the fullness of the Gentiles will come to its close before the times of the Gentiles are terminated. Accepting the usual interpretation that the church, the body of Christ, will be caught up with Christ to glory before the time of tribulation predicted for Daniel's seventieth week, it seems clear that the fullness of the Gentiles will come abruptly to its close when the church is caught up to heaven. If so, we have here the terminus of the fullness of the Gentiles and the terminus of Israel's blindness.

TWO ASPECTS OF ISRAEL'S RESTORATION

A problem frequently overlooked by premillennial writers

who accept the solution of Romans 11:25 given above is that the Scriptures do not confirm any immediate change in "all Israel" after the rapture. During the tribulation period it is only a remnant which turns to Christ. It seems clear that the majority of Jews as well as Gentiles will worship the beasts of Revelation 13 instead of Christ, and that the Jews will re-establish their ancient worship in Jerusalem in unbelief rather than in acceptance of their Messiah. How then is Israel's blindness lifted?

The answer seems to be that the restoration of Israel is in two major steps. At the rapture of the church, Gentiles again take second place in God's program and the Jew resumes his place. It is a time of Gentile domination but not of Gentile blessing. The unfulfilled program of the seventieth week of Daniel is completed during the final period before the second coming of Christ. During this period among unbelieving Jews, the Mosiac laws and sacrifices are reinstituted. As far as Israel as a whole is concerned, there is no evidence of a large turning to Christ. During this time, however, a remnant will turn to Christ. Apparently the very act of the rapture of the church serves to confirm to those who are honestly seeking their Messiah, howbeit in blindness, that Jesus of Nazareth is the true Messiah and the only Savior. Overnight, after the church is caught up, many of Israel have their eyes opened to the truth and immediately become the evangels of the period. The special blindness which was Israel's judgment during the time of Gentile blessing is removed, and the Jew resumes his place.

The language of Romans 11:25 in this connection must be carefully noted. While it is revealed that the special blindness peculiar to Israel is lifted, the passage does not reveal any distinct enlightenment. The Jew is restored to an equal place with the Gentile in the matter of discernment of the gospel rather than to a place of greater privilege. The release, such as it is, will undoubtedly occasion a great turning to Christ among Israel after the rapture of the church, but by no means is the entire nation won to Christ. The Scriptures are relatively silent on the details, but there is evidence that a remnant will turn to Christ (cf. the 144,000 of Revelation 7) and that many do not turn to Christ (cf. the re-establishment of sacrifices and the Mosaic worship). While the special blindness of Israel is therefore lifted at the time of the rapture of the church, Israel is still in the same difficulty as the Gentiles in that they are naturally blind to the gospel and dead in sin. Apart from the work of the Holy Spirit in this period, certainly essential to salvation them as now, none of Israel would be saved even after the blindness is taken away.

The consummation of God's purpose in delivering Israel from their special blindness is found in the remnant that greets Christ at His second coming. It seems clear that before Christ returns Israel will turn to Him and will formally acknowledge their sin. Zechariah 12:10 speaks of this:

> "And I will pour upon the house of David, and upon the inhabitants of Jerusalem, the spirit of grace and of supplication; and they shall look unto me whom they have pierced; and they shall mourn for him, as one mourneth for his only son, and shall be in bitterness for him, as one that is in bitterness for his first-born."

The passage goes on to describe the mourning and the cleansing from sin that follows. It is apparently the divine preparation for the return of their Messiah. In the days of the awful tribulation of Israel, in which their ancient worship is once more prescribed and all natural Jews become the objects of persecution, there will undoubtedly be many more of Israel brought to Christ through the personal work of those previously saved. While many of the Gentiles will also be brought to Christ

(Rev. 7:9-14), this period will be a special time for Jewish evangelism and it will be climaxed by the outpouring of the Spirit of God as a preparation for the return of Christ. The second phase of Israel's restoration is accomplished thus at the end of the tribulation, while the first phase occurs at its beginning.

The chief significance of Romans 11:25 does not, however, lie in its details. The important fact is that it indicates a termination of the present age of Gentile blessing in the gospel and the preparation of Israel for a future period. Any interpretation of the passage which deals with the terms in their ordinary meaning demands a system of prophecy which allows for a future for Israel. The consummation of Romans 11:25 is described in the verses which follow: the national salvation of Israel, the coming of the Deliverer out of Zion, and the fulfillment of God's covenant with His ancient people.

Chapter VIII

THE FUTURE RESTORATION OF ISRAEL

THE CONFUSION in the minds of expositors of Scripture concerning the meaning of Romans 11:26 is one of the evident results of failure to use Biblical interpretation. Not only do various schools of thought disagree, but the passage is a problem to all. An important clue to its interpretation is found in its preceding context. The entire chapter of Romans 11 deals with the question, "Did God cast off His people?" (Rom. 11:1). The answer given to this leading question is that "God did not cast off his people which he foreknew" (Rom. 11:2).

The argument proceeds to point out that there has always been a remnant of Israel who believed both under the law and under grace. The fact that this group were only a small portion of the nation of Israel is explained as the occasion for the present grace extended to Gentiles: "I say then, Did they stumble that they might fall? God forbid: but by their fall salvation is come unto the Gentiles, to provoke them to jealousy" (Rom. 11:11). The argument then turns on the statement that if the unbelief and "fall" of Israel as a nation was the occasion of blessing on the Gentiles, how much more will be the blessing on both Gentiles and Israel when Israel comes into its fullness of blessing: "Now if their fall is the riches of the world, and their loss the riches of the Gentiles; how much more their fulness?" (Rom. 11:12). These facts combine to serve as a warning to Gentiles not to be high-minded and as an encouragement to Israel that a future time of blessing is in store.

The contrast throughout the passage is not between the believer and unbeliever, but between Gentiles as such and Israel as a nation. In Romans 11:25 the issue is brought to a head with the revelation that Israel's present blindness and unbelief will be concluded at the same time that the present Gentile opportunity is ended. Then follows the event described as "all Israel" being delivered.

The issues involved in the passage under consideration can be resolved into a series of questions: (1) What is the meaning of "all Israel"? (2) What is the nature of the deliverance? (3) When will the deliverance occur? (4) What are the concomitant events? Any answer to these questions involves both premises based on interpretation of the entire Scriptures and exegesis of the passage itself. The history of its interpretation has revealed a tendency to determine the meaning of the passage largely on the basis of other Scriptures. Hence, most amillennialists have denied that the reference is to Israel in the flesh and have given a spiritual interpretation of the passage. Premillennialists have insisted upon a more literal exegesis. The issue is determined by the meaning of key words.

WHAT IS THE MEANING OF "ALL ISRAEL"?

It is apparent that the construction placed upon the word *Israel* practically determines the exegesis of the entire passage. The question is answered by at least three important considerations: (1) What is the use of the word in the context? (2) What is the use of the word in the New Testament as a whole? (3) What is the relation of the question to doctrine in general?

A study of the context bears out the fact that the word *Israel* as used in this passage is in contrast to *Gentile*. This is clear in Romans 11:1, where Paul identifies himself as an Israelite because of his connection with the tribe of Benjamin—a racial and national relation rather than spiritual. The contrast is made further in Romans 11:11 ff. The use of "ye"—i.e., the Gentiles—is opposed to "they"; i.e., the Jews. In other words, the entire chapter carefully preserves the distinction between two classes: Jews and Gentiles. Further, the Gentiles are in most cases those who have believed in Christ and are members of the church. The contrast is not, therefore, between believing Israel and unbelieving Gentiles, but rather the two groups are treated racially. There is no ground whatever in this passage for the idea that Israel is a reference to all believers as such, the interpretation advanced by Origen, furthered by Calvin, and embraced by most amillennialists. This interpretation would nullify the very theme of the chapter.

The immediate context also brings out the contrast between Israel and Gentiles. In Romans 11:25 both terms occur in contrast. As far as the general context and the immediate context are concerned, there is no ground for spiritualizing the word *Israel.* Even A. T. Robertson, who is not a premillennialist, rather reluctantly admits that the context would indicate that the reference here is to the Jewish people.[1] Charles Hodge, who is also not a premillennialist, states flatly, "Israel, here, from the context, must mean the Jewish people, and *all Israel,* the whole nation. The Jews, as a people, are now rejected; as a people, they are to be restored."[2] The amillennial view that Israel refers to all believers must be held in spite of the context. It is noteworthy that Oswald T. Allis, who more than any other recent amillennial writer has attempted formally to refute premillennialism, passes by Romans 11:26 with only a footnote reference[3] in which he tries to sustain his thesis that Romans 11 says nothing of Israel's

---

[1]A. T. Robertson, *Word Pictures in the New Testament,* IV, 398.
[2]Charles Hodge, *Commentary on the Epistle to the Romans,* p. 589.
[3]Oswald T. Allis, *Prophecy and the Church,* p. 305.

restoration.[4] In brief, his argument is that if Paul believed in Israel's restoration he would have mentioned restoration *to the land*. In other words, because Paul does not include all the elements of Israel's restoration, he cannot be speaking on the subject at all. If words are to be taken in their ordinary meaning, Paul is speaking of Israel's spiritual and national restoration throughout the chapter. The fact is that Romans 11:26 is an embarrassing passage to the amillennial school of interpretation and, as they have no satisfactory interpretation of it, they are prone to give none.

The predicament of the amillennialists in interpreting Romans 11:26 is further disclosed by examination of their theory that *Israel* as a term is constantly used in the New Testament as a synonym of the church composed of both Jews and Gentiles. Their prejudice is expressed well by Allis when he states that when the Brethren Movement "insisted that Israel must mean Israel, and that the kingdom promises in the Old Testament concern Israel and are to be fulfilled to Israel literally" that they were "carrying to an almost unprecedented extreme that literalism which is characteristic of Millenarianism."[5] Yet Allis himself admits that premillennialism "was extensively held in the Early Church."[6] and that it was superseded only when Augustine advanced the idea that the millennium was "to be interpreted spiritually as fulfilled in the Christian Church."[7] As a matter of fact even a casual study of the writings of the early fathers reveals that millenarianism was not only "extensively held" but was in fact the outstanding characteristic of early Christian eschatology. Wilbur Smith in his review of Allis' books quotes Schaff to this effect:

[4] *Ibid.*, p. 100.
[5] *Ibid.*, p. 218.
[6] *Ibid.*, p. 7.
[7] *Ibid.*, p. 3.

"The most striking point in the eschatology of the ante-Nicene age is the prominent chiliasm, or millenarianism, that is the belief of a visible reign of Christ in glory on earth with the risen saints for a thousand years, before the general resurrection and judgment. It was indeed not the doctrine of the church embodied in any creed or form of devotion, but a widely current opinion of distinguished teachers, such as Barnabas, Papias, Justin Martyr, Irenaeus, Tertullian, Methodius, and Lactantius."[8]

Allis' "unprecedented literalism" was, in the impartial hands of doctrinal historians, the prevailing opinion of the church until the perversions of Augustine and Roman Catholicism began to have weight. After all, is it such "unprecedented literalism" to believe that the Bible means Israel when it uses the term? Is not the burden of proof on the amillennialist to prove that the word means other than its ordinary meaning?

It is not difficult to prove from Scripture that *Israel* is frequently used in the New Testament to mean what it meant in the Old Testament—the nation descending from Abraham through Jacob. Further, *there is not a single reference in the New Testament to Israel which cannot be taken in its plain meaning. Not a single instance requires the term to include Gentiles.* In a word, there is no justification based on usage in the New Testament to interpret the word *Israel* as ever including Gentiles.

The question remains concerning the relation of the passage to Biblical doctrine as a whole. This involves the issues which determine premillennialism and amillennialism as systems of doctrines—a subject which is too large to be treated here. This much is clear: the premillennial system of interpretation is in full harmony with the interpretation that *Israel* in this passage refers to Jews in the flesh rather than to all believers, Jews and

[8]*The Sunday School Times*, Nov. 24, 1945, p. 940.

Gentiles alike. The amillennial system demands that the passage
be spiritualized or their whole system is in jeopardy. The nature
of the argument is illuminating, however. The amillennialist
usually argues that Israel must be spiritualized because to do
otherwise involves what is to him the extreme literalism that
Israel means Israel. In other words, he argues from the system
of doctrine to its necessary interpretation of the passage. On
the other hand, the premillennialist appeals to the immediate
context—in contrast between Israel and Gentiles; the general
context—the discussion of Gentile privilege because of Israel's
fall; and the usage in the New Testament as a whole. From the
standpoint of arriving at Biblical doctrine, the hermeneutics of
the premillennial argument is evidently sound.

A difficulty for all systems of interpretation is the use of the
word *all*. What is meant when it is stated that "all Israel shall
be saved"? This has been referred to as a difficulty of the premillennial interpretation. Obviously, all Israel are not saved.
Israel in view in the prophecy must first of all be limited to
living Israel; that is, those living on earth at the time. It is not
true that all Israelites of all generations are to be saved. Further,
the Scriptures reveal that a large portion of Israel will be martyred
during the time of trouble preceding the consummation of the
period before the second coming of Christ (Zech. 13:8-9). There
are other complications in the doctrine when the judgment on
Israel is taken into consideration (Ezek. 20:33-38). What is
meant, then, by *all*?

Before attempting to answer the question, it should be noted
that the same difficulty attends the amillennial view, or any
other view which attempts to find an actual event in this passage.
While *Israel*, according to the amillennialist, means "all believers,"
it is also apparent that all believers are not saved at the end of
the age by the coming of Christ. For the proper interpretation

of the passage, both principal millennial views must limit the fulfillment to those living at the time. The difficulty is not, then, a result of the premillennial viewpoint.

The most evident answer to the question of the meaning of *all* is found in the context. The *all* is in antithesis to the *in part* of Romans 11:25 and the *remnant* of verse 5. During the present age a remnant of Israel is saved through the gospel. The hardening or blindness is "in part." When Christ returns, the situation will be changed. Instead of a remnant, or a small part, Israel as a whole will be saved. It will be a national deliverance. A. T. Robertson while attempting to defend postmillennialism in his interpretation admits: "*All Israel* (*pas Israel*). What does Paul mean? The immediate context (use of *pas* in contrast to *apo merous, pleroma* here in contrast with *pleroma* in verse 12) argues for the Jewish people 'as a whole.' "[9] He goes on to express his opinon that other Scripture (Rom. 9:6; Gal. 6:16) may justify the teaching that both Jew and Gentile or "spiritual Israel may be the idea."[10]

The opinion of Charles Hodge is worthy of weight as he is not arguing for premillennialism: "Israel, here, from the context, must mean the Jewish people, and *all Israel,* the whole nation. The Jews, as a people, are now rejected; as a people, they are to be restored. As their rejection, although national, did not include the rejection of every individual; so their restoration, although in like manner national, need not be assumed to include the salvation of every individual Jew. *Pas Israel* is not therefore to be here understood to mean, all the true people of God, as Augustine, Calvin, and many others explain it; nor all the elect Jews, i.e., all that part of the nation which constitutes

---

[9]*Op. cit.*, p. 398.
[10]*Loc. cit.*

'the remnant according to the election of grace'; but the whole nation, as a nation."[11] The viewpoint that "all Israel" means "Israel as a whole" is not "an almost unprecedented extreme" of "literalism which is characteristic of Millenarianism,"[12] as Allis would have us believe, nor is it a peculiarity of a little sect of Plymouth Brethren. It is the interpretation of those who believe that Israel means Israel, whether premillennial or post-millennial, and it is the only interpretation which makes sense out of the eleventh chapter of Romans. William Hendriksen, formerly Professor of New Testament Literature at Calvin Seminary and an avowed amillennialist, interestingly disagrees with Allis and holds that *all Israel* refers to the total number of Elect Israel in all ages; i.e., holds to a literal interpretation of the passage. This is, to say the least, an improvement on Augustine, Calvin, and Allis, though it misses the point of the context.[13] The deliverance predicted in Romans 11:26 is, clearly, a group deliverance rather than individual salvation. This is borne out in the explanation which follows in the chapter.

WHAT IS THE NATURE OF THE DELIVERANCE?

The salvation of "all Israel" is described as a fulfillment of prophecy. Isaiah 59:20-21 is quoted in part in Romans 11:26-27. The full quotation in Isaiah is as follows:

> "And a Redeemer will come to Zion, and unto them that turn from transgression in Jacob, saith Jehovah. And as for me, this is my covenant with them, saith Jehovah: my Spirit that is upon thee, and my words which I have put in thy mouth, shall not depart out of thy mouth, nor out of the mouth of thy seed, nor out of the mouth of thy seed's seed, saith Jehovah, from henceforth and for ever."

[11]*Op. cit.*, p. 589.
[12]*Op. cit.*, p. 218.
[13]*And So All Israel Shall Be Saved*, p. 33.

Three things are mentioned specifically in the Romans quotation: (1) the Redeemer shall come *out of* Zion; (2) He shall turn ungodliness from Jacob; (3) this is a covenant to be fulfilled "when I shall take away their sins."

All views of the millennium agree that the Deliverer is the Lord Jesus Christ. Question has been raised concerning the meaning of "out of Zion." The Hebrew of Isaiah 59:20 is correctly rendered "to Zion." The Septuagint has interpreted this to mean "for Zion" (*eneken Zion*). Paul in quoting the Hebrew uses neither the Hebrew nor the Septuagint when he quotes the passage as "from Zion" (*ek Zion*). How is this difficulty to be solved and what is the meaning of *Zion*? It is clear that Paul is here not directly quoting, but is gathering up various passages in one statement. It will be noticed that his reference to turning away ungodliness is not in the Isaiah passage either. The Scriptures speak of Christ as both coming *to* Zion and *from* Zion (cf. Ps. 14:7; 20:2; 53:6; 110:2; 128:5; 134:3; 135:21; Isa. 2:3; Joel 3:16; Amos 1:2). It is certainly quibbling with words to argue, as Allis does, that this change of wording favors the amillennial view that a heavenly city is intended.[14] In the nature of the case, Christ must come "to Zion" before He comes "from Zion." The deliverance promised Israel is not His second coming *per se,* but His rule on earth after His coming.

What is meant by *Zion*? This term has been used in reference to the city of Jerusalem or parts of it "at least since the time of David."[15] A study of its usage in the Old Testament reveals that its meaning is literal; that is, it is always associated with the earthly Zion. Its use in the New Testament is also literal. The only cases in question are the references in Hebrews 12:22 and Revelation 14:1, which readily yield to a literal inter-

---

[14]*Op. cit.,* p. 305.
[15]"Ziou," *International Standard Bible Encyclopaedia.*

pretation if the premillennial viewpoint be adopted in interpreting the passages as a whole. In no case does Zion become
merely a "heavenly city."[16] The many predictions in the Old
Testament foretelling the coming of the Deliverer "out of Zion"
(see references above) argue for a literal interpretation.

When the Deliverer comes, He will "turn away ungodliness
from Jacob." This is an event, not a process extending over
ages of time. It is the subject of much Old Testament prophecy.
It is part and parcel of the new covenant which Romans 11:27
mentions. A classic Old Testament passage bearing on the subject is Jeremiah 31:31-37. A new covenant is promised the house
of Israel. In this new covenant, Jehovah promises:

> "I will put my law in their inward parts, and in their heart
> will I write it; and I will be their God, and they shall be
> my people. And they shall teach no more every man his
> neighbor, and every man his brother, saying, Know Jehovah;
> for they shall all know me, from the least of them unto the
> greatest of them, saith Jehovah: for I will forgive their in-
> iquity, and their sin will I remember no more" (Jer.
> 31:33-34).

The passage then goes on to declare that Israel will endure *as
a nation* under this new covenant as long as the ordinances of
the sun, moon, and stars endure. The passage concludes: "Thus
saith Jehovah: If heaven above can be measured, and the
foundations of the earth searched out beneath, then will I also
cast off all the seed of Israel for all that they have done, saith
Jehovah" (Jer. 31:37). In brief, the new covenant promised the
house of Israel is precisely what Paul refers to in Romans 11:26-27.
The elements are the same: Israel is promised blessing as a
group or nation; "all" are to be blessed; "all" are to know the
Lord; "all" are to be forgiven. Certainly, this is not the picture

---

[16]Allis, *op. cit.*, p. 305.

of Israel in any period of its history until now. A literal fulfillment demands an interpretation of Romans 11:26-27 which is
in accord with the premillennial position. The fact that believers
in this age enjoy a "new covenant" of grace and blessing does
not hinder the future fulfillment of this promise to Israel, which
is in no wise being fulfilled now.

The premillennial interpretation of Scripture adds a great
deal to the bare outline provided in Romans 11:26-27. According
to this viewpoint, the deliverance will be more than spiritual.
Israel will be in the great tribulation and threatened with extermination (Matt. 24:15-22). Christ at His coming will deliver
them from physical harm. This is in view of their coming
spiritual blessing which will be their portion after being judged
and brought into the land of promise. These events are the
means to the end—the spiritual blessing on Israel throughout
the millennium. To argue that all the details of the complicated
series of events which will bring Gentile power to its end and
establish the kingdom of Christ on earth must be in this portion
of Romans in order to establish the premillennial view of the
future, is an example of the error of arguing from silence.[17]

When Will the Promised Deliverance Occur?

The amillennial viewpoint of Romans 11:25-26 among other
things does manifest injustice to the chronology of the passage.
Whether the view of traditional amillennialism be followed, or
the recent view of Hendriksen that "all Israel" refers to elect
Israel in all ages, the interpretation contradicts the order of events
indicated in Romans 11. The point of the entire chapter is that
the present age is one of blessing to Gentiles and that this follows
Israel's fall. During this age some in Israel come to Christ and
are saved, but the nation as a whole goes on in hardness or

---
[17]Loc. cit.

blindness and in unbelief. According to Romans 11:25-26, the present situation is going to change when the fullness of the Gentiles, or the present period of Gentile blessing, comes to its close. The terminus of Gentile blessing is the point in time when Israel's blindness is lifted. When Israel's blindness is lifted, the way is opened for the work of the Deliverer who will bring spiritual restoration as well as physical. The order of events is therefore: (1) Israel's fall; (2) Gentile fullness of blessing; (3) Israel's blindness lifted; (4) Israel's Deliverer comes out of Zion; (5) Israel is turned away from ungodliness and her covenants are fulfilled. Now, manifestly, Israel fell as a nation. The reference is not to believing Israel or true Israel. Likewise, Israel is blind as a nation, but believing Israel is not blinded even in this age. So also "all Israel" refers not to believers in this age or in any previous age, but to the entire group which enter the millennium. To make "all Israel" "all believers," as Allis does, or "all Jewish believers," as Hendriksen does, is to blur the distinctions which are so carefully maintained in the entire passage. A study of the entire chapter, including verses 28-32, reveals that the antithesis of "ye" and "they," i.e., present believers as in contrast to "all Israel," is carefully preserved throughout.

The deliverance of "all Israel" is not a process but an event. The time of the event is clearly when the Deliverer comes out of Zion, an event following the return of Christ in His second coming. The prophesied deliverance is, therefore, a future event and a single event. The great prophetic passages of the Old Testament upon which this prophecy is based do not have any harmony with the present undertaking of God. It is evident that it is not true today that everyone knows the Lord, that it is no longer necessary to teach our neighbors. This is not true for Gentiles and it is certainly not true for Israel. The future revelation of Christ to Israel will fulfill these predictions and bring the prophesied time of blessing for God's ancient people.

WHAT ARE THE CONCOMITANT EVENTS?

The predictions of Romans 11:25 ff. involve important doctrinal considerations beyond the revelation explicitly made. This explains why its interpretation has been characterized rather sharply by the school of interpretation represented. The premillennial interpretation has as its background important considerations. The restoration of Israel as a nation involves the Davidic covenant. It involves Israel's continuance as a nation and possession of the land. It involves the separation of the purposes of God for the church, believers in this age, and for Israel. The themes of Scripture bearing on the time of great tribulation for Israel, the consummation of Gentile power, the second coming of Christ, the judgment of the Gentiles, the resurrection of Israel and her judgment, the judgment of Israel still in the flesh, and many other important doctrines are directly or indirectly related. It is not claimed that Romans 11 in itself settles all the problems or that it alone establishes the main premises of premillennialism. What is claimed is that a literal interpretation of Romans 11 is in full harmony with prophecy which has been and is being fulfilled and that it fits perfectly the general scheme of the premillennial interpretation of Scripture. If the statements of this chapter be taken in their ordinary meaning without recourse to allegorical or spiritual interpretation of the key words, the inevitable conclusion is that we have here in broad outline God's program: present blessing for Gentiles, future restoration and blessing for Israel as a nation. We say with Paul in the sense we believe he meant: "Did God cast off his people? God forbid."

CHAPTER IX

PREDICTED DIVINE JUDGMENTS

THE CERTAINTY OF DIVINE JUDGMENTS

THE SUBJECT before us is a very serious one and also a comprehensive one from a doctrinal standpoint. The Scriptures tell us plainly in Hebrews 9:27 that "it is appointed unto men once to die, but after this the judgment." This means that every soul anywhere in all the world, past, present, or future—every human being who has ever walked the face of the earth—some day will stand before a holy, omniscient, all-powerful God who will judge according to the standard of perfect righteousness. This makes the doctrine very personal. Theologians who believe the Word of God, regardless of their viewpoint concerning the millennium, are agreed that there is appointed to every man a time of judgment before God, and that this is certainly going to take place in God's future program for the world and for the individual. Those who believe that the Bible teaches a specific program of events understand that this judgment will not be one general judgment as viewed by some theologians. Instead of being one judgment in one place with one set of circumstances, it is a series of judgments, some of which are separated from the earlier judgments by the whole millennial period of one thousand years. The predicted divine judgments, then, while they extend to every soul, are not judgments which all take place in one moment of time.

THE JUDGMENT AT THE CROSS

The fact is that one of God's great judgments is already

past. That judgment is the judgment of Christ as the "Lamb of God, which taketh away the sin of the world," and it took place on Calvary more than nineteen hundred years ago. The moment we really trusted in Christ our judgment for the guilt of sin became effective once and for all. It was accomplished for us at the cross of Christ. For a Christian there is no future judgment for sin. There is no future condemnation for sin, "for there is no condemnation to them which are in Christ Jesus."

The Judgment Seat of Christ

For a Christian there is only one future judgment and that is the judgment at the judgment seat of Christ, which is a judgment of works in which Christians will be rewarded according to what they have done, whether it be good or bad. The central passage of the Bible on this subject is 2 Corinthians 5:8-11. In this portion of Scripture Paul writes to the Corinthian church:

> "We are confident, I say, and willing rather to be absent from the body, and to be present with the Lord. Wherefore we labour, that, whether present or absent, we may be accepted of him [literally, 'be well pleasing to him']. For we must all appear before the judgment seat of Christ; that every one may receive the things done in his body, according to that he hath done, whether it be good or bad. Knowing therefore the terror of the Lord, we persuade men; but we are made manifest unto God; and I trust also are made manifest in your consciences."

This passage presents, first of all, the fact that all Christians will stand before the judgment seat of Christ. The basis for this judgment is not going to be the question of whether we are saved or lost. It is very plain that the issue of whether one is saved or lost is not settled in eternity future; it is settled right here and now by what one does with Jesus Christ. That is finished before one leaves this world. Everyone in this judgment is already saved and it is only a question of rewards.

When we come before God, if our life could be viewed as a ledger sheet with its credits and its debits or with its good works and its bad works, it is only a question of classification; and when we come before God the debit side is absolutely clean. It is all wiped out. The question is, What is there to our credit? As the books are examined, if we may use that figure of speech, we are rewarded according to our works.

There are three figures in the New Testament used to illustrate this truth. The first figure is found in Romans 14:10-12, where it is used of our life as a stewardship. A steward is a servant to whom is committed a trust and he has to report to his master. On the basis of this, our lives are viewed as a stewardship and the argument is raised: "Why dost thou judge thy brother? or why dost thou set at nought thy brother? for we all stand before the judgment seat of Christ. For it is written, As I live, saith the Lord, every knee shall bow to me, and every tongue shall confess to God" (Rom. 14:10-11). The point of this passage is that we are declared to be stewards. This same figure is brought out in 1 Corinthians 4:1-5, particularly verse 5, where we are told to judge nothing before the time that God judges our lives. In other words, everyone of us, as stated in Romans 14:12, "shall give account of himself to God." As a steward reports to his master, so God is going to hold us accountable in that day for what He has committed to us. We have a great many things committed to us. We all have life; we have spiritual gifts; we have opportunities; we have power; we have money; whatever we have God has given to us. There is no ground for pride, for everything that is good has been given to us by God. The more one has the more he has to give account for in that day of judgment.

In 1 Corinthians 9:24-27 the figure is used of an athletic contest, a runner striving for the prize, and we are exhorted so to run that we may obtain. Life is a race. We are to live in such a way that when we stand before Christ we will win the prize.

One of the most comprehensive figures is found in 1 Corinthians 3:11-15, where the illustration of a building is used. This portion of Scripture presents the Christian life as built upon the foundation of salvation. "Other foundation can no man lay than that is laid, which is Jesus Christ." In other words, God supplies the foundation upon which we build. According to the context, we can use six different materials: gold, silver, precious stones, wood, hay, and stubble. No doubt, each of these materials has its spiritual meaning, but the important point is that the gold, silver, and precious stones are fireproof, whereas wood, hay, and stubble are all consumed by fire. We are warned very faithfully that fire is going to try every man's work of what sort it is. Verses 14-15: "If any man's work abide [or remain] which he hath built thereupon, he shall receive a reward. If any man's work shall be burned, he shall suffer loss: but he himself shall be saved; yet so as by fire."

Now it is made very plain that we are not saved by the house we build. We are saved because we are on the foundation. We are on the foundation if we are trusting in Jesus Christ as our personal Savior. But the life we are building on that foundation will be subject to judgment, represented by fire which will test our lives according to eternal values. The gold, silver, and precious stones may not make a big and showy house, but they stand the test of fire. The wood, hay, and stubble will erect a big building, but they burn very easily. There is a very obvious point to this: What kind of a building are we building? The only kind of building which is worth while is a fireproof building—a life that is lived in the will of God to the glory of God. We will have some great surprises in eternity. Some people may have built a lovely house of wood. They may have used the best of wood, such as mahogany. They may have polished it and carved it until it was just the acme of all that human ability could do. But when the test of fire comes, it will be reduced to ashes just as the hay and the stubble. There are different degrees of value and worth here, but the important thing is the fact that we will some day stand before Christ and everything that is not of eternal value will be reduced to ashes. We are going to be rewarded according to that we have done for the Lord.

It is a wonderful token of grace that no one is going to be lost in this judgment. "If any man's work shall be burned, he shall suffer loss [the whole building destroyed]: but he himself shall be saved; yet so as by fire." We occasionally read in the paper of someone who is awakened in the night to find the house on fire and flees in his nightclothes, and has the agony of seeing everything he owns go up in smoke. Tragic, is it not? But that is what some are doing spiritually. When they leave this world they are going to have nothing to take with them. It may not be quite that bad. According to 1 Corinthians 4:5, the forecast is that when our life is judged, "then shall every man have praise of God." Every Christian is going to have a little left. God is not going to ruin all our building. But how important it is as we face that judgment to have a life that is well spent in the Lord's service. Some people talk about prophecy being impractical. There is no more practical prophetic truth than this simple pointed doctrine of the judgment seat of Christ. When we stand in that judgment, the Scripture states clearly that we will stand before a judge who knows all about us.

I sometimes try to press home, while teaching theological

students, how important it is to have a Christian home and to
live in that Christian home a Christian life. One is no better
Christian than the person who knows him best thinks he is.
Where does that put you? What does your husband think of
your spiritual testimony? Parents, what do your children think
about your spiritual testimony? Children are some of the best
judges to be found anywhere. One does not deceive them.
When we stand before God, we are going to stand before the
Lord Jesus Christ who knows us better than any human frame
can know us. How important it is to extend to every relationship of life, to every contact, the fragrance and the love of
Christ! We should manifest in all our relationships that sweet-
ness of Christian testimony which Christ said should characterize the Christian life: "By this shall all men know that
ye are my disciples, if ye have love one to another." As people
come in contact with us, they should see more than orthodoxy;
they should see more than zeal; they should see the beauty of
Christ. As we stand before Christ in that day, this is the thing
that will be so very, very important.

This subject embraces the whole of Christian life: soul
winning, prayer life, giving, sacrifice, work, everything. All
is involved. As we stand before Christ, we are going to have
a perfectly just judgment. We will get our whole pay. Sometimes in this life we do not get paid in full. Sometimes we are
overpaid. But there is an equalization board in heaven. When
we get up there, we can be sure that all inequities will be fully
corrected. In that day many missionaries who have turned their
backs on comfort, home, and friends here in this land and have
labored under great difficulty and opposition of Satan, encounter-
ing loneliness and difficulty of every sort, will be paid in full.
How wonderful it will be in that day when they stand before
the Savior who loved them and gave Himself for them!

JUDGMENT OF THE GENTILES

When Christ comes back, there will be at least two major judgments. These concern not the resurrected dead nor the translated, but the living in the world at that time. The judgment of the Gentiles (Matt. 25:31-46) has created some concern and misapprehension on the part of God's people. If you are a Christian, you do not need to worry about this judgment because you will not be included with those judged here. It concerns those who are living on the earth at the time Christ returns to establish His kingdom. In Matthew 25:31-32 it is revealed: "When the Son of man shall come in his glory [the time is specified, the second coming of Christ], and all the holy angels with him, then shall he sit upon the throne of his glory: and before him shall be gathered all nations: and he shall separate them one from another, as a shepherd divideth his sheep from the goats." The passage goes on to describe what follows. The sheep are ushered into the millennial kingdom, and the goats are cast into everlasting fire.

There are some very important questions raised by the study of this portion of Scripture. First of all, who are the nations? There has been, unfortunately, some confusion here, partly due to the translation in the Authorized Version by the word *nations*. That is exactly the same word translated many times in the Bible by the word *Gentiles*. No doubt God will judge nations as such throughout the tribulation time as judgment after judgment will be poured out upon the nations of the world. When it comes to this judgment, however, by its very nature it must be an individual judgment. People are going to stand before God not in the mass but as individuals. Therefore, this word should have been translated *Gentiles,* as it is in Matthew 6:31-32 and in 20:19

where it predicts concerning Christ, "And shall deliver him to the Gentiles to mock, and to scourge, and crucify."

In this portion of Scripture there are three different classes of people: "my brethren," the sheep, and the goats. Judgment upon the sheep and the goats will be according to their treatment of "my brethren." The brethren are not brought into judgment here. Not a word is spoken about their being judged. No mention is made here of anyone being raised from the dead. No resurrection is in view in this Scripture. It is not a general judgment. It has to do only with the Gentiles living in the world at the time Christ returns.

The basis of the judgment has confused some people. Seemingly, it is a judgment based on works, and the question is naturally raised, "Is anyone in any dispensation ever saved by works?" You will notice when the King sets the sheep and the goats before Him He says to those on His right hand, who are the sheep: "Come, ye blessed of my Father, inherit the kingdom prepared for you from the foundation of the world: for I was an hungred, and ye gave me meat: I was thirsty, and ye gave me drink: I was a stranger, and ye took me in: naked, and ye clothed me: I was sick, and ye visited me: I was in prison, and ye came unto me" (Matt. 25:34-36). The righteous answer, "When did we do this?" And He replies: "Inasmuch as ye have done it unto one of the least of these my brethren, ye have done it unto me." In other words, it is on the basis of works. How can these people be ushered into the kingdom on a basis of works? The goats are judged on the same basis. They are caused to depart into everlasting fire because they did not do these things.

It is plainly taught in Scripture that the only ground for salvation in any dispensation is grace. In other words, all the Old Testament saints were saved because of the fact that Christ was going to die. This is the teaching of Romans 3:25 where it is stated that the basis for God's forgiveness to Old Testament saints was the fact that God knew that Christ was going to die and pay for their sins on the cross. The Old Testament saints were saved, as it were, on credit. We today have just the opposite situation. We look back to the payment on the cross and we are saved by what Christ did nineteen hundred years ago. In the tribulation time and in the millennium, everyone who is saved will be saved on the basis of what Christ did for him on the cross. But why then these works?

If we examine the Scriptures, we will find that in different dispensations there are different outward tokens of faith. For instance, examine an Israelite in the Old Testament in regard to the question of whether he is saved. How would you know? If you watched him and found him carefully, conscientiously keeping the law of Moses, bringing his sacrifices, doing the things that the law prescribed, you would say he was saved. He would be saved not because he kept the law but because keeping the law was the outer evidence of a work of God in his heart which we call salvation. In the present age we are told that faith without works is dead. Why? Because faith without works is not real faith. Faith cannot be seen. It is an immaterial thing. All one can see is the evidence of it. In the present age, when we try to determine whether a person is saved, we may first of all try to get a testimony from him concerning his relationship to the Lord Jesus Christ. We may form a judgment about whether he is saved or not on the basis of what he says. Or we may watch his life. We may form a judgment as to whether he is saved on the basis of what he does. What he says and what he does cannot save him. God, who sees the heart, knows whether he is really trusting in Christ.

In Matthew, chapter 25, while the emphasis is on works, it

is the emphasis on works as a testimony to the fact that those being judged are saved. In the time of awful tribulation which these people will come through, there will be a strong spirit of deceit on the part of Satan. People will be deluded. They will believe a lie. There will be a sharp contrast between those who trust in God and those who do not. And in that period of time particularly the whole world will be gripped by a hatred for the Jews which will be inspired by Satan himself. Anyone who does not hate the Jew in that time (and with the very risk of his life will befriend the Jew to the extent of visiting him in prison and showing his interest in him) will do so only for one reason and that would be that he had had vital dealing with the Lord Jesus Christ. In this present age, sometimes unsaved people do very kind things and very courageous things. In the tribulation time, no one will do what this Scripture says the sheep do unless they are really trusting in Christ.

The Scripture promises that the sheep will enter the kingdom, but the goats will be cast into everlasting fire. Some consider the everlasting fire equivalent to the lake of fire. The present state of the unsaved is fire, and it will be everlasting in its character, but not until after the judgment of the great white throne are the unsaved cast into the lake of fire. Fire characterizes the state of the lost immediately upon death and is therefore everlasting.

The Judgment of Israel

The Scriptures reveal that the brethren, or Israel, will also be brought into a place of judgment. This judgment is described in Ezekiel 20:34-38. The context indicates that God is, first of all, going to gather Israel out of all countries at the second coming of Christ:

"I will bring you out from the people, and will gather you out of the countries wherein ye are scattered, with a mighty hand, and with a stretched out arm, and with fury poured out. And I will bring you into the wilderness of the people, and there will I plead with you face to face. Like as I Egypt, so will I plead with you, saith the Lord GOD. And I will cause you to pass under the rod, and I will bring you into the bond of the covenant: and I will purge out from among you the rebels, and them that transgress against me: I will bring them forth out of the country where they sojourn, and they shall not enter into the land of Israel: and ye shall know that I am the LORD" (Ezek. 20:34-38).

This passage teaches that at the time of the second coming of Christ He will gather every Israelite from all over the world and bring them into this central meeting place, and there He will judge them on the issue of whether they are saved or not. The rebels, or unbelievers—those who continue to blaspheme against God, who have rejected the Lord Jesus Christ—will be purged out as unfit to enter the kingdom. But those who are left are the remnant, the godly remnant of Israel, who in that awful hour of the tribulation found that Christ was their Messiah indeed and their Savior, and turned to Him and trusted Him. In this judgment God separates saved from unsaved at the beginning of the millennium. Due to the fact that unsaved Gentiles and unsaved Jews are purged out, the millennial period will begin with only saved people.

The world in that day will be a very wonderful world. Saved people, people who came to know Christ in the fiery crucible of the tribulation, who counted the cost, who were willing to die if need be for their faith in Christ, will be rewarded by entering the glorious, wonderful millennial period when Christ will reign over them. During the thousand-year period these who have come through the tribulation are still in the flesh. They still have mortal bodies and will till the ground, tend their farms, and beget children. There will be a tremendous increase in population through the thousand-year period so that at the end of the millennium the world population will be greatly increased with the millions of people who will have been born during that period. These will be subject to the judgments which come at the close of the millennium.

At the close of the millennium Satan will be loosed and permitted once again to deceive the nations. Some of these born in the millennium will follow Satan and rebel against God as recorded in Revelation 20:8-9. They will gather against the camp of the saints (Rev. 20:9). The judgment of God then will come upon them as fire descends from God out of heaven and devours them. They will suffer physical death in this way.

THE JUDGMENT OF THE GREAT WHITE THRONE

After the conclusion of the millennium, according to Scripture there is a great white throne established (Rev. 20:11) ."And I saw a great white throne, and him that sat on it, from whose face the earth and the heaven fled away; and there was found no place for them." The present earth and the present starry heavens will be destroyed at the end of the millennium and this judgment will take place in space. It is not related either to heaven or to earth and the Scriptures declare in verse 12: "I saw the dead, small and great, stand before God; and the books were opened; and another book was opened, which is the book of life: and the dead were judged out of those things which were written in the books, according to their works."

Every predicted divine judgment, whether it deals with saved people or lost people, is according to works. The judgment of the Gentiles is according to works. The Jew is judged according to whether he has rebelled against God or not. At the great white throne, they are judged out of those things which are written in the book according to their works. What does that mean? It means that every soul in one way or another will stand before God and be judged according to his works: but there is a tremendous difference in the principle of each of these judgments. For the Christian the question is, What has he done for Christ? What are his rewards? What are his crowns? But for the lost it is not a question of reward, but of punishment. What has he done against God? What does he merit in just judgment from God? The Scripture states that they were judged every man according to his works. "And the sea gave up the dead which were in it; and death and hell delivered up the dead which were in them: and they were judged every man according to their works. And death and hell [the temporary place of the dead] were cast into the lake of fire. This is the second death. And whosoever was not found written in the book of life was cast into the lake of fire" (Rev. 20:13-15).

These are solemn words, but they are just as true as John 3:16, or any precious promise ever claimed in the Word of God. These verses are the Word of God. Christ said that not one jot or tittle can pass from the law until all is fulfilled. The Word of God is eternal; it cannot be broken; it must be fulfilled. These sad words are going to be fulfilled. "Whosoever was not found written in the book of life was cast into the lake of fire." The judgment of the great white throne concerns lost souls only. There are some people in Scripture concerning whom we have no revelation. For instance, there must be somewhere a final judgment of those who go through the millennium. The judgment of the Gentiles and the judgment of the Jews at the beginning of the millennium were not final judgments for them. There apparently is a judgment of rewards for them that is not revealed to us because it does not concern us. There will no doubt be further instruction given to the millennial saints while Christ is reigning on earth.

The judgment of the great white throne, however, concerns this present generation. Everyone whose name is not written in the book of life, according to this Scripture, will be cast into the lake of fire. That does not mean extermination. According to the Scripture, this is the eternal state of those who know not Christ. This passage raises the important question, Where are you going to spend eternity? Those who know the Lord Jesus Christ as personal Savior will not be at this judgment of the great white throne. They will be judged at the judgment seat of Christ and will receive rewards. They will be with the Lord forever in a place of bliss and grace where God's love is free to manifest itself to them for all eternity. What a wonderful state it is to be saved! If we are saved, we never have ground for complaining about anything. It is so wonderful that it transcends every other thing that may occur to us in life.

For the unsaved, however, it can be said on the authority of the Word of God that unless they receive Jesus Christ as their Savior they will be cast into the lake of fire at this awful final judgment. This is plain as the Word of God can make it. When Christ was on earth He said a great deal more about punishment and eternal punishment than He said about heaven. He was faithful in warning His generation that they were not dealing simply with theological concepts but with the destiny of their own souls.

THE PRESENT OPPORTUNITY

It is of God's grace that it is not too late. The Scriptures state, "Now is the accepted time." Right now it is possible to settle this issue for all eternity, if in the heart there is the willingness to receive Jesus Christ as personal Savior. God will not save one against his will, but He will save anyone who is willing to trust in Christ.

There are four simple facts regarding God's divine judgments. First of all, the judgment of God is universal. It deals with both men and angels, though the judgment of angels has not been considered in our present study. No one escapes divine judgment. That means everyone of us will some day be judged by Christ Himself.

The second fact is that the judgment of God is absolutely certain. There is no question about it. We are not gambling about the future. We are dealing with absolute certainty. We will face Christ and He will be our judge. The Scriptures make this perfectly clear.

The third fact is that the judgment of God is just. If God saves one for all eternity it will be just, because Christ died. If God rewards one it will be a just compensation. There will be no favorites, for God is perfectly just.

The fourth fact is that the judgment of God is based upon the principle of human responsibility. God holds us responsible for our opportunity, for our life, for all that of which He has made us stewards. Sometimes it is supposed that grace relieves us of responsibility. It does not. It increases it. Grace emphasizes the whole matter of our responsibilty to God. We are responsible for grace. We are responsible for our gifts, for our possessions, for our thoughts, for our love, for our opportunities for worship, for our faith, for everything God has given us. When we face the Lord Jesus Christ, may it be a gracious judgment, a judgment of reward, a judgment of blessing, a joyous time of compensation for lives that have been spent in the Lord's service. But if there should be one reading this message who has never trusted in

Christ, may I invite you to receive in simple faith the Lord Jesus Christ as your God and Savior. God will save your soul for eternity and give you His wonderful salvation if you will only trust in Christ.

CHAPTER X

THE FUTURE OF COMMUNISM
ACCORDING TO THE BIBLE

THE SUBJECT of Communism occupies the minds and hearts of more people today probably than any other subject. No doubt, there are millions of people who are seeking the answer to the question, What is the future of Communism? Everyone recognizes that Communism has had large part in our current history. Much of what is happening in the world is related directly to Communism.

When facing the future, there are few questions in our day that are more important in the secular field than the future of Communism. Millions of dollars are being spent by various governments of the world, using all the devices which the human mind can conceive, in order to trace a future course for Communism. One can hardly pick up a paper or a magazine which does not have an article on the subject.

COMMUNISM IN RELATION TO AMERICA

The questions we have about Communism are near to our hearts because we are asking, even here in America, What is the relationship of Communism to our great country? Are we going to be embraced by Communism? Are we facing a radical change in our living standards? Are we going to face some of the bloody purges which have overtaken other countries of the world? Certainly anyone who is willing to think realizes that we have a real problem in Communism in the world. Before our eyes in recent years we have seen Communism advance, embracing great numbers of people in a movement that is absolutely unprecedented in all the history of the race.

At the present time there are some 800,000,000 people under thet control of Communistic type governments. We recognize that this is a tremendous portion of the earth's population and a movement unparalleled in history. If we are alert to the time in which we live, it is very natural for us to ask, What is the future of Communism?

PLAIN FACTS ABOUT COMMUNISM

I do not have access to top secret information in Washington, nor do I speak in the role of an expert on Communism. We do not need unusual sources of information to chart the course of Communism. All of us have learned much about Communism in recent years. Communism is more than a form of government; it is more than mere propaganda on the part of Russia; it is more than just a philosophy of the "have nots" trying to get the possessions of those who "have."

About ten years ago I was taking a graduate course in history under the head of the history department in one of our large universities. In one of his lectures, the professor remarked that Communism would never come to America. His reason was that America was too prosperous. He labored under the idea that Communism was only for poor ignoramuses. Anyone who has learned something about Communism will find that not only people in poverty but many who are wealthy have been converts to Communism. Some of our leading Communists are intellectuals—people who have property, ability, and keen minds. What is there in Communism that attracts such people?

As we study Communism in the world today, we find it is more than a mere economic theory. It is a movement built upon blasphemy against God. It denies that God exists and embraces as its very heart what we call atheism. Communists do not believe that there is any such being as a supreme God. Along with this are the other elements of Communism with which we are quite familiar. One of those other elements is materialism. Communists tell us the only real things in the world are material things. The supernatural or the spirit world does not exist for them. They assert that the world is moving inevitably to a goal which is Communism, and that capitalism will be replaced by a Communist society regardless of what we do about it. They believe in what is sometimes called "economic determinism." They hold also that forces are let loose in the world which inevitably will plunge the whole world into a communistic society.

THE BIBLE AN IMPORTANT DOCUMENT ON COMMUNISM

Most of us have heard all of these things many times. As we face these questions, and what the Communists themselves say concerning the future, we as Christians come back to the one Book in all the world which reveals the future of Communism. If you want the inside story on Communism, turn to the inside of your Bible.

There are three lines of truth in the Bible which lead to certain definite conclusions regarding the future of Communism. These lines of truth are built upon some comprehension of the prophetic Word. Many Christians have studied the Bible and know something of the broad purposes of God. Building upon this background, we may know what the Word of God says about the future of Communism.

RUSSIA WILL NEVER DOMINATE THE WHOLE WORLD

First of all, the Bible makes clear that we are in the midst of a planned program to which Christ referred in Luke 21:24 as "the times of the Gentiles"—a period of time which began about six hundred years before Christ and, according to the Word, will continue until Christ comes back. It is revealed in chapters 2 and 7 of the Book of Daniel that in this period there will be five great world governments. Daniel speaks first concerning the world empire of Babylon headed up by Nebuchadnezzar, which conquered Jerusalem and destroyed it approximately six hundred years before Christ. Both Scripture and history tell the story that Babylon was succeeded by a second great world government known as the kingdom of the Medes and Persians. The record of the downfall of the Babylonian Empire in the fifth chapter of Daniel is substantiated by secular history. Later Alexander the Great, king of Greece, came on the scene. His rapid conquest of the world of his day, prophesied in detail in the eighth chapter of Daniel, is familiar to all students of history.

The Book of Daniel pictures a fourth great world empire, which is not named, as following Alexander. According to history, this is none other than the great Roman Empire which was in power at the time our Lord was born in Bethlehem. The Romans had control of most of the civilized world. It was the world empire of its day.

As the Book of Daniel presents these four great world empires, it states clearly that the Roman Empire will be succeeded by a fifth empire. This fifth empire will have God Himself reigning over it (Dan. 2:44-45). A study of what Daniel has to say, compared with the other prophets and such portions of Scripture as Revelation 20, will lead rightly to the conclusion that the fifth world empire is none other than the world kingdom of our Lord and Savior Jesus Christ which premillenarians identify with the millennial kingdom which Christ will bring into the world when He returns in power and great glory as the Scriptures prophesy.

Christians living today, however, find themselves in an age which Daniel did not anticipate except perhaps by implication. A careful study of Daniel 9:24-27 will indicate that a period of time is implied between verses 26 and 27. This period is not described by Daniel, and is uncharted as far as the Old Testament is concerned. It occurs before the seventieth "week" of Daniel 9:27, the last seven-year program leading up to the second coming of Christ.

The previous program of Daniel 9:24-26 has been very carefully carried out, embracing 69 sevens of years followed by the death of Christ which occurred "after" the close of the sixty-ninth seven and before the beginning of the seventieth seven or "week." From the death of Christ down to this present day, however, there has been no advance whatever in the fulfillment of Daniel's prophecy, indicating that Israel's program has been set aside while another program is being completed.

Many students of the Scriptures have come to the conclusion that God in this present age is carrying out a purpose not revealed to Daniel, and that purpose is to call out from every nation and kindred and people a group to be known as "the church," the body of Christ—those who are trusting in Jesus Christ as Savior in this day and age and who are being baptized into the body of Christ by the Holy Spirit. God has continued this program to the present hour and it will continue until Christ comes for His church, at which time the dead in Christ are resurrected and the living church is translated into heaven as recorded in 1 Thessalonians 4:13-18. All of these wonderful truths are a part of the prophetic Word, but the important thing for us to realize is that, according to Daniel's prophecy and the truth revealed in the Book of Revelation, the last seven years of "the times of the Gentiles" are still ahead. That period of seven years will begin, we believe, shortly after the church is taken home to glory, an event which many regard as imminent in the sense that it could occur any day.

The order of future events include, then, the coming of Christ for His church and the fulfillment of the last seven years of Daniel's prophecy for Israel. In this seven years the fourth or Roman Empire, contemplated by Daniel, is revived and brought to its destruction at the second coming of Christ. Following this, the fifth world empire—the millennial kingdom of Christ—is brought into being. While it would be naive to claim that all students of the Bible accept this interpretation, it is commonly held by premillenarians and those who have specailized in the study of prophecy.

If this outline of future events can be accepted as the Scriptural revelation, we can come to a few important conclusions. According to Daniel's prophecy, there is no room for another world empire except the one which the Bible mentions as the revival of that fourth world empire. After the church has been translated and taken to heaven, this empire will be revived. It is revealed that there will be a confederacy of states around the Mediterranean area similar to the ancient Roman Empire which in God's view will be a continuation of that fourth empire. The fourth empire eventually will become a world government and a dictator will head this revived Roman Empire who will rule over the entire world. Nevertheless, there will be only four world empires. The fifth will be the millennial kingdom of the Lord Jesus Christ.

These simple facts, quite familiar to many Christians, point to the truth that the Scriptures allow for no other world empire than those already mentioned. *Russia as a military power can never gain control of all the world*. There is nothing in the

Word of God which would lead us to the conclusion that Russia will be able to create a world power. In fact, a study of Matthew 24:6-8 reveals that the present age is a period "of wars and rumours of wars. . . . Nation shall rise again ration, and kingdom against kingdom." If that is the situation, and it certainly has been ever since Christ was on earth, it is also clear that there can be no world government worthy of the name in this present church age. The only world government before the second coming of Christ is the predicted revival of the fourth empire which does not come until after the translation of the church.

We can learn this also from the study of history. Many have attempted a world government. Napoleon tried, but he came to his end at Waterloo. Germany tried twice for world domination, but failed. Japan entered World War II with the same dream of world dominion, particularly of the Orient, but Japan failed. From the time of Christ to the present, there has been no other world government than that one which was in the world when Christ came and died—the Roman government. As far as the Scriptures reveal the course of the present age, they point to the conclusion that it is impossible for Russia or for any other nation to achieve a world government of a real character during this present age of grace.

RUSSIA HEADED FOR MILITARY DISASTER

A second important line of truth is found in chapters 38 and 39 of Ezekiel. Much has been written and said concerning this passage of Scripture which reveals the great battle of Gog and Magog. Most Bible students who have attempted to interpret the passage literally have come to the conclusion that in these two chapters there is portrayed a future military invasion of the land of Palestine by a great army which sweeps down from the north. Ezekiel begins with this pronouncement in which God speaks of the people who will participate in the invasion:

> "The word of Jehovah came unto me, saying, Son of man, set thy face toward Gog, of the land of Magog, the prince of Rosh, Meshech, and Tubal, and prophesy against him, and say, Thus saith the Lord Jehovah: Behold, I am against thee, O Gog, prince of Rosh, Meshech, and Tubal: and I will turn thee about, and put hooks into thy jaws, and I will bring thee forth, and all thine army, horses and horsemen, all of them clothed in full armor, a great company with buckler and shield, all of them handling swords" (Ezek. 38:1-4, A.S.V.).

The verses following speak of the other nations which will be a part of this great army.

The Scriptures also declare that this army will come from the north, and will come upon the land of Palestine in a period that is described here as a period of security for the nation Israel. Ezekiel 38:14-16 states:

> "Therefore, son of man, prophesy, and say unto Gog, Thus saith the Lord Jehovah: In that day when my people Israel dwelleth securely, shalt thou not know it? And thou shalt come from thy place *out of the uttermost parts of the north,* thou, and many peoples with thee, all of them riding upon horses, a great company and a mighty army; and thou shalt come up against my people Israel, as a cloud to cover the land: *it shall come to pass in the latter days,* that I will bring thee against my land, that the nations may know me, when I shall be sanctified in thee, O Gog, before their eyes" (A.S.V., italics supplied).

It seems clear according to this word of Scripture that this army will come from the north. If the terms are traced—such as "Rosh" which is close to the word *Russia,* and "Meshech" which many say refers to the city of Moscow—a clear identification can be made in this portion of Scripture of a great army coming down from Russia upon the land of Palestine. This is confirmed by the fact that the army comes from the north.

Furthermore, the time of the invasion is described in two sentences: it is first declared specifically to occur in "the latter days," and then, also, it is described as occurring in a time "when . . . Israel dwelleth securely." Israel is not dwelling securely, or at rest, today in any real sense of the word. We all know of the tension which exists in the land of Palestine. Prophecy reveals that, after the church has been taken home to glory, the head of the revived Roman Empire is going to enter into a contract with the Jewish people. In that agreement he is going to offer them protection with the result that Israel will return to Palestine in even greater numbers than we have seen in recent days. They will dwell securely, not because they have an army of their own, but because they are under the protection of this Gentile ruler. Apparently, the battle that is pictured in Ezekiel 38 will occur during the first half of that last seven-year period leading to the second coming of Christ to establish His kingdom in the world, possibly just preceding the beginning of the last three and one-half years, called the "great tribulation."

Chapter 39 of the Book of Ezekiel reveals what happens to this army. Verses 1-4 state:

" . . . Behold, I am against thee, O Gog, prince of Rosh, Meshech, and Tubal: and I will turn thee about, and will lead thee on, and will cause thee to come up from the uttermost parts of the north; and I will bring thee upon the mountains of Israel; and I will smite thy bow out of they left hand, and will cause thine arrows to fall out of thy right hand. Thou shalt fall upon the mountains of Israel, thou, and all thy hordes, and the peoples that are with thee: I will give thee unto the ravenous birds of every sort, and to the beasts of the field to be devoured" (A.S.V.).

The passage goes on to mention the fact that these hordes will be almost completely destroyed.

Here is something that would really make news. If today the military might of Russia were suddenly destroyed, we can be sure it would be most dramatic news. According to the Word of God, that very thing will occur. As a result of the slaughter of the Russian army by a judgment from God, there will be a sudden shift of military power. With Russia out of the way, the head of the revived Roman Empire, in control of the Mediterranean area at that time, will be able to proclaim himself as dictator of the whole world. .There will be, accordingly, a fulfillment of the Scriptures which prophesy that the Roman government of that time will not only rule over all the territory of the ancient Roman Empire, but will extend its suzerainty to every people, land, kindred, and tongue (cf. Rev. 13:4-8). Chapters 38 and 39 of Ezekiel may well fit into the prophetic picture, and the defeat of Russia and its miliary force may be the occasion of the establishment of the world government by the world rulers pictured in Scripture. If this point of view is correct and our interpretation of these passages sustained, certain definite conclusions can be reached.

If it is necessary in that day for Russia to move into the land of Palestine in order to attempt to conquer it by military force, it should be obvious that Russia then will not be in control of the entire world. In fact, Russia's position at that time will be apparently very similar to what it is now—a great military power but *not* in control of the whole world. In other words, instead of being a world conqueror, Russia, according to the prophetic Word, will be defeated at that time and put down as a military power. If this is the case, we can easily see how the events which have led us to the present hour have been a divine preparation for the consummation of the age. If one believes that the Lord may come for His church at any moment, these prophecies can be fulfilled in the following order:

1. The church will be taken to heaven.
2. The Mediterranean area will be organized into a united states or confederacy of nations headed up by a ruler, the "prince that shall come" (Dan. 9:26).
3. Under these circumstances, Russia will attempt to conquer the land of Palestine, but will miserably fail and its armies will be destroyed.
4. Then, the revived Roman Empire will extend and exercise power over the entire world until destroyed by Christ in His second advent (Dan. 2:44-45).

All of these events are portrayed in the Word of God and subject to future fulfillment. Concerning the question of the future of Communism, the Word of God points definitely to the conclusion that Russia will never conquer all the world. As far as the Bible is concerned, there is no room for a world government by the Russian armies.

COMMUNISTIC GODLESSNESS DESTINED TO BE WORLD-WIDE

However, there is a third line of truth which is the most important part of this study. The Scriptures seem very clear that Russia, as a political power, will never dominate the world, powerful as it is today. But there is plain teaching in the Bible concerning the continuation of that form of godlessness which is found in Russia. We find in our present generation an unparalleled phenomenon in the entire history of the world in the *religious* character of the communistic system. It has been pointed out that Communism is basically a religion. The unusual thing about it is that this kind of religion is not confined to Russia and it would not die if Russia were destroyed. Communism is based upon a godless philosophy, that is, materialism or a belief that there is no God.

In examining in the Scriptures the picture of the religious character of the future time of the great tribulation, it is observed that there is an amazing similiarity to the religious character of Communism as it exists today. In fact, the same kind of materialistic blasphemy against God which characterizes Communism today will be carried over into the religion of the Antichrist. While Communism will not be perpetuated as a political movement, it apparently will be perpetuated as a religion.

This is confirmed by a study of Daniel 11:36-39. In this passage a revelation is given concerning the king who will come. This king is none other than the head of the revived Roman Empire and, as such, he is the one who is destined to be the dictator of the whole world. The description of this king given in Daniel 11:36 is as follows:

> "And the king shall do according to his will; and he shall exalt himself, and magnify himself above every god, and shall speak marvellous things against the God of gods; and he shall prosper till the indignation be accomplished" (A.S.V.).

This passage teaches that the king not only exalts himself above man, but actually exalts himself above every god. Verses 37-38 describe the religious system that will be characteristic of that time:

> "Neither shall he regard the gods of his fathers, nor the desire of women, nor regard any god; for he shall magnify himself above all. But in his place shall he honor the god of fortresses; and a god whom his fathers knew not shall he honor with gold, and silver, and with precious stones and pleasant things" (A.S.V.).

What may be learned from this portion of Scripture? It teaches that the absolute ruler of the world in the time of the coming great tribulation will have a form of religion that is practically identical to what is found in modern Communism. Russia is the first great nation in all history which has embraced atheism—a denial of God—as its official religion. The world ruler here, described as this king, will have a similar kind of religion described as honoring "the god of fortresses." Just what is "the god of fortresses"? It is military power personified. That is the only god Communism has—military power. Communists worship power, and this future world dictator will worship power also. Such will be the character of his religion.

A companion passage to Daniel in the New Testament is Revelation 13. In this chapter we have a picture of the same person, now described as the "beast out of the sea," the one who is going to rule over the whole world. The passage reveals how he will receive his power from Satan who is portrayed as the dragon. The question is asked: "Who is like unto the beast? and who can make war with him?" This question relates to military power. As indicated above, the god of that day will be a god of military power, a god of materialism, and a god utterly contrary to the Christian faith. This person will continue for forty-two months. He begins the world-wide character of his reign at the time of the beginning of the great tribulation. At that time he sets himself up as the world dictator and takes power over the entire world. He will continue for the last three and one-half years preceding the second coming of Christ to establish His kingdom. The character of this evil person is described in Revelation 13:6-8 (and one can almost hear the blasphemy of Communists as these verses are read): "He opened his mouth in blasphemy against God, to blaspheme his name, and his tabernacle, and them that dwell in heaven. And it was given unto him to make war with the saints, and to overcome them: and power was given him over all kindreds, and tongues, and nations. And all that dwell upon the earth shall worship him." The beast will thus become the object of worship of the whole world and be the embodiment of military power.

This portion of Scripture and the companion portion in Daniel 11 lead to some very important conclusions relative to the question of the future of Russia and the future of Communism. The Scriptures make clear that Russia, as a military power, will never dominate the world, and therefore we can expect the Scriptures to be fulfilled which anticipate that Russia will be crushed in that future time. But there is one thing in Communism which will continue and that is the religion of materialism. After the church is taken home to glory the same kind of blasphemy, unbelief, and rebellion against God as characterizes the communistic movement today will seize the world as a whole and be headed up in this one world ruler. It is obvious that this dictator will not rule as Communism does today. It is the rule of one man whereas Communism is not. This world dictator will be an absolute monarch, but his rule will be characterized by an atheism and a materialism which denies God just as Communism does now.

As we face Communism in our day, we need not fear that as a political force it will dominate the world. We should use every means to contain it and to keep it from spreading, but it is quite apparent according to the Word of God that, as a political system, it will never conquer the world.

But we do have something to fear, and even Christians, intelligent in the Word of God, do not always understand the implications of Communism. Our real enemy is not Russia, and neither is our real enemy Communism. Our real enemy is the atheistic blasphemy that is behind it. It is the unbelief

in God and in Christ, and a turning away from belief in the
God of the Scripture. Here in America it is necessary for us
to fight Communism. It is necessary for us to arm in order
to protect ourselves as a nation. Nevertheless, our real enemy
is not Communism, nor a political theory. Our real danger is the
godlessness and the atheism of our day. Some will say there are
not very many people who are atheists. Perhaps not, at least
they are not the kind who stand on soap boxes and proclaim
atheism. But there are many today who are living in practical
atheism; living as if God did not exist; living as if there
were no heaven, no hell, no judgment, and no divine reckoning
with human sin. Yes, America's real enemy is not Communism.
It is the blasphemous unbelief in God behind Communism that
is our true enemy.

How to Fight Communism

What conclusions may we draw from these facts as Christians? Certainly we need to oppose Communism in every way
we can. But what is our approach? What is the demand God
puts upon us in this hour? What can we do? Thinking Christians will recognize that we need to come to God in prayer for
the crisis of our present day. Certainly our hearts should go
out to the millions who are in trouble and suffering and fear
behind the iron curtain, to those many thousand Christians who
are standing true, even though they may seal their testimony with
their own blood. Yes, for many these are tragic hours as far as
suffering is concerned. But what is the demand upon us? What
can we do in the face of encroaching unbelief as we see it in the
world today.

First of all, one of our best answers is to do what God has
called us to do: proclaim the gospel to the ends of the earth,
engage in evangelism and in the missionary program of the

church, and send out ambassadors of the cross. One of the best ways to counter Communism is to preach the gospel. If a fraction of the effort that is being put into our military machine could be diverted to a true preaching of the gospel, we should begin to see the tide turn even in our day.

Certainly, we need Bible teaching in our day. If a person is led to trust in Jesus Christ as his Savior and in the Word of God, one does not fear that he will become a Communist. Communism and Christianity, true Christianity, do not mix. If a man felt that it was his life mission to combat Communism and the various ideas involved in it, the best way to do it would be to preach the gospel and to use whatever means were at his disposal for disseminating the good news concerning Christ as the One who loved us and died for us. Certainly we need churches; we need missions; we need Christian schools—every method that God can use to send out the gospel in this day of His grace.

Then, as we face the question of the future of Communism, may we turn to a question that is even more important: What is our own future? The Scriptures seem to indicate that the future of Communism is not too bright, that Russia as a nation is destined sooner or later to fall, and that God is going to bring into judgment the blasphemy and unbelief that characterizes much of our day. But the real question for each one of us now—and that should burn into our souls—is: Where do I fit into God's future program? What is my future? Do I know that if I should be taken from this world God would take me home to glory because I have trusted in the Lord Jesus Christ as my personal Savior? Have I been saved through faith in Him and His blood which was shed for me on the cross? In this day of grace, have I availed myself of the love and mercy of God by trusting in Jesus Christ as my personal Savior? Yes, the Scriptures reveal the future of Communism, but the Scriptures also tell us much more concerning the future of individual hearts and lives of those who have trusted in Christ, and also the future of those who have not.

Friend, if you have not trusted in Christ, may I appeal to you to take Him as your personal Savior? You can *know* your future, whatever the future of the world may be. You can know that you are safe forever if you are willing to trust in Jesus Christ as your own Savior.

Chapter XI

CAN WE HAVE PEACE IN OUR TIME?

The Longing for World Peace

FEW SUBJECTS have been pondered more in our day than the question, Can we have peace in our time? This topic is being considered not only by Christians but by adherents of every type of religion, every type of belief or unbelief, and every type of political persuasion. It is not limited to the United States, nor to any color or culture. The whole world is seeking peace. All that is needed to have a headline on the front page of our papers is to have some Russian official smile a bit over something or other and immediately there is a wave of optimism that peace is around the corner. It reveals how close this matter is to the hearts of many people in the world.

The Need for World Peace

In America, however, the need of peace has been only partially realized. We are remarkably comfortable and smug in this country. Most of us do not know what it is to be without homes, without food, and without any hope of the future as far as this world is concerned. No conqueror has ever come to our homes and told us to get out with only the clothes on our backs and to abandon all our earthly possessions. We have never lost our children through separation while fleeing from an enemy. But, in spite of the fact that we have suffered so little in comparison to many millions of the earth, even in America there is longing for peace. Nothing is more universal in the world today than the longing for peace.

NEED FOR PEACE IN THE HEART

Not only is there longing for peace politically, but if one examines the faces of people as they hurry along their way many of them tell the unspoken story of a longing for peace, for rest of heart, and for the lifting of some burden or trouble. There is much sorrow and difficulty even in our nation where we are blessed with so many material things. Peace of heart is a wonderful fruit of the Holy Spirit which is possible for believers in Christ. Even if war should come, Christians could have peace. This fact, so significant in itself, only emphasizes the need for world peace. Can the God who gives peace to the heart also give peace to the world? Can we have peace in our time? What does the Bible teach?

BIBLICAL PROPHECY OF WORLD PEACE

It is well to recognize that the Bible says a great deal about peace. It is unfortunate that many Christians do not know what the Bible teaches on this subject. Many passages in the Bible speak of a coming time when the nations of the world will be at peace one with the other. For instance, in Psalm 72 there are many references to peace which predict that the Lord Jesus Christ will bring peace at His second coming. In verse 3 it is revealed, "The mountains shall bring peace to the people, and the little hills, by righteousness." It is recorded in verse 7 of this Psalm that "In his days shall the righteous flourish; and abundance of peace so long as the moon endureth." It is clear that the Bible definitely predicts a time of peace.

In Isaiah, chapter 2, there is another promise of peace in

relation to the time when the Lord will come to Zion. In Isaiah 2:4 it is written: "He shall judge among the nations, and shall rebuke many people: and they shall beat their swords into plowshares, and their spears into pruninghooks: nation shall not lift up sword against nation, neither shall they learn war any more." This definite promise of world-wide peace is connected with the coming of the Lord. Another important reference is found in Isaiah 9:7 concerning the Son to be given to Israel, "Of the increase of his government and peace there shall be no end." This is another sure promise of peace on the earth. These passages could be multiplied as they are not isolated references. There are many predictions in the Old Testament of the time of peace, a time when nations will give up their instruments of war and turn them into instruments of peace.

WHY ARE PROPHECIES OF WORLD PEACE UNFULFILLED?

Why have these Scriptures predicting world peace not been fulfilled? Why is it that today, instead of beating our swords into plowshares and our spears into pruninghooks, we in America are spending seventy percent of our total national income on what we call defense, military weapons, and the upkeep of our military forces. The answer is that the world situation demands it. We need to defend ourselves. But it is a confession of the sense of insecurity that grips the hearts of leaders and populace alike. There is no peace in sight except an armed peace. Why is it that the peace predicted in the Bible has not come to the world?

The answer to this question is quite clear. The Scriptures reveal that the peace which is promised the world is connected with the coming of the Messiah who is the Lord Jesus Christ. History records the sad spectacle that when Christ came to the world, born of the Virgin Mary, and delivered His message to men, proclaiming Himself to be the Messiah of the Jews and the Savior of the world, the answer of the world was "Crucify him, crucify him!" There on the hill of Calvary our Lord and Savior was crucified between two thieves. Thus the One who alone could give peace was rejected. Why do we not have peace? The answer is that we do not have Christ. He alone is the Prince of peace.

What Can We Do?

A very natural question is "What can we do?" The Old Testament had this problem, as well as the New Testament. In the Old Testament Israel longed for peace and did not have it because they were not willing to yield their hearts and lives to God. They were not willing to believe the Word of God. As a result, many sad trials came to them. They were warned that they would lose their homes, be led off into captivity, and be separated forever from their children. They experienced all these pangs of heart because they were not willing to let God have His way. The prophets accordingly exhort the people to turn back to God. In 2 Chronicles 7:14 a typical word of exhortation and promise is given: "If my people, which are called by my name, shall humble themselves, and pray, and seek my face, and turn from their wicked ways; then will I hear from heaven, and will forgive their sin, and will heal their land."

This promise was given to Israel under the Old Testament order of things. In the Old Testament God said in effect: "If you want peace, come, confess your sins, yield your heart to me, obey my law, and I will heal your land." In the Old Testament Israel was given specific promises. God told them: "If you obey me; I will give you peace; I will prosper you; I will cause your crops to prosper; I will give you rest among your enemies; I will keep you from pestilence and from disaster." If they did not obey, God said that He would pour judgment after judgment upon them (Deut. 28—30). In spite of the plain warning of the Word of God, Israel turned its back on God. The result is recorded in historical sections of the Old Testament.

No Peace Without God

While the promises of the Word of God addressed to the Christian are somewhat different than those given Israel, it is clear that today, as yesterday, one cannot have peace without God. If one is looking for peace, he will not find it unless he finds it in God and in Christ. This is the only place where one can find peace. God is the author of peace, not man. How can man expect to have peace when he is at war with the Almighty God? The Scriptures, then, are perfectly plain why the world is in chaos today. The world is trying to get along without Christ. No amount of military arms will ever give us peace. It may serve as an expedient. We recognize the necessity of armed might, but it will not bring peace. Only Christ can bring peace. There will be no peace, according to the Scriptures, until Christ brings it.

Signs of World Peace

Christ was once asked an important question by His disciples. They were concerned about the fact that the kingdom promises had not been fulfilled. The kingdom to them was the kingdom of righteousness and peace predicted in the Old Testament. They wanted to know when this would come, when the end would come of the age in which they were living, and when He was going to inaugurate this glorious kingdom. In Matthew 24 Christ gave them various signs, the things that would happen before the kingdom came to pass. One of the signs was mentioned in Matthew 24:6-7: "Ye shall hear of wars and rumours of wars: see that ye be not troubled: for all these things must come to pass, but the end is not yet. For nation shall rise against nation, and kingdom against kingdom: and there shall be famines, and pestilences, and earthquakes, in divers places." Christ described in these words the character of the period between His first and second comings. This will also be the character of the time of awful tribulation and trouble predicted in Scripture. War will continue right up to the day the Prince of peace comes to establish peace.

Is There a Practical Program for Peace?

The question is raised, What can we do about it? We must be practical about a program for peace. As long as we are living in a wicked world, there is some need for having armies and for spending money for defense. Few would recommend the abolishing of the police forces in our cities. It is recognized that while a police force should not be necessary, nevertheless there is a need for it under present conditions. Force must be used in order to maintain order in a wicked world. Likewise, in the world as a whole every effort should be made to maintain world peace.

On the other hand, there will not be any lasting peace for this world resulting from military force. We are merely putting crutches under a weak and sick world. It may stand up for a few more days, but it is not going to cure the disease. There is something fundamentally wrong with the world. It will be in war and trouble and turmoil until a new world order comes. This cannot be fulfilled until Christ returns and sets up His kingdom. Then, and then alone, nations of the world will abandon their instruments of war. Then only there will be peace and tranquillity over all the world for a thousand years when Christ will reign on the earth.

PEACE FOR TODAY

But what can be done about peace today? A very practical program concerning peace is revealed in the Scriptures. There is nothing man can do that will change fundamentally the course of world history. We are quite helpless to accomplish anything in the world except through prayer.

However, there is a way of peace which God has made wonderfully simple. It is a way of peace for the individual who is living in a war-torn world where uncertainties are the normal thing. While the future is unknown as far as ordinary history is concerned, there is a way of peace provided for us through the Lord Jesus Christ.

In that wonderful fifty-third chapter of Isaiah, our Lord Jesus Christ is pictured in His rejection and in His death by crucifixion as the Lamb of God sacrificed for us. In verse 5, it is written: "He was wounded for our transgressions, he was bruised for our iniquities: the chastisement of our peace was upon him; and with his stripes we are healed." There is a way of peace which has been bought by the precious blood of Christ. The Lord is able to bring peace with God for the sinner who is estranged, who is under God's righteous judgment, and is without hope and without God. Peace is provided for the sinner who deserves to die, who deserves to be punished, and who does not have any merit. Christ died, and because He died there is a way of peace.

In Colossians 1:20 there is reference to this same truth in relation to Christ: "Having made peace through the blood of his cross, by him to reconcile all things unto himself; by him, I say, whether they be things in earth, or things in heaven." Again in Romans 5:1, it is written: "Therefore being justified by faith, we have peace with God through our Lord Jesus Christ."

The greatest question in all the world as far as peace is concerned is not the question as to whether we can get along with Russia, or whether there will be another world war or not. These may be great questions, but they are not the greatest question. The greatest question is whether we have peace with God.

THE ONLY WAY OF PEACE

The Bible makes it clear that the only way one can have peace with God is through faith in Jesus Christ. If we have trusted in Jesus Christ as our personal Savior and if we have accepted what Christ did for us on the cross, we can have peace. It is promised to us, "Being justified by faith, we have peace." It is a present possession. The enmity is wiped out. The judgment is gone. We are at peace with God because we are accepted in the perfection of the person and work of His dear Son.

Oh the wonder and the joy of knowing that we have peace with God in spite of our unworthiness. Can we have peace in our time? We may not have peace with nations, but we can have peace with God. Peace with God is the position of every Christian. It is not so much an experience as it is a fact. One is either at peace with God or he is not at peace with Him. If one is saved, he has peace with God.

PEACE AS THE GIFT OF GOD

After one has peace with God, there is also the possibility of a vital experience of peace. Some Christians have peace *with* God who know very little about the peace *of* God, which is the experience of peace.

The Scriptures, however, speak of this aspect of peace frequently. In John 14:27, Christ was dealing with His disciples on the night before His crucifixion. The disciples were fearful.

They did not know what the future held. They had sensed that something was impending, but they did not know what it was. They did not know that Christ would be crucified the next day. He had told them he was going to die, but they had not believed it. The Scriptures indicate that they were troubled. He had said in John 13 that He was going away, but they could not understand. In 14:1 He exhorted them, "Let not your heart be troubled," but they still were perplexed. Now He tells them in verse 27: "Peace I leave with you, my peace I give unto you: not as the world giveth, give I unto you. Let not your heart be troubled, neither let it be afraid."

Do you have the peace of God? It is God's gift. You cannot earn it, and no amount of resolve on your part can secure it. It is something God has to do for you. In Galatians 5:22, we are told that the fruit of the Spirit is love, joy, peace. The thing that astounds us is not that Christ simply gives us peace, but He said, "My peace I give unto you" (John 14:27). "My peace"! What is the peace of Christ? What is He talking about on this night before His crucifixion? Twenty-four hours later His body lay in a tomb, riven with the nails in His hands and feet, the spear wound in His side, and yet He speaks of "my peace." What kind of peace is this?

None of us, of course, understand the peace of Christ. We cannot enter into the consciousness of the incarnate Son of God. But what did Christ mean when He said "My peace I give unto you"? How could Christ, knowing what was ahead for Him, have peace at this time? He knew that He would die on the cross the next day.

The peace of Christ, as nearly as we can define it, is the rest of heart that is God's own experience. God has perfect confidence in His own wisdom, power, and love so that He knows that all things will work together for good to them that love

God. The only way, then, one can have the peace of God is to attain perfect confidence in the God who gives peace. When one realizes that he is trusting One who is infinitely wise and powerful, who knows all about everything, who has perfect provision for every human need, then he can have peace. When one realizes that his life is in the hands of a God who loves him enough to send His Son to die for him, and that the Christ who died is risen and is interceding for him at the right hand of the Father, then he can have peace. When one believes that God has promised never to let him go until God has perfected His work and he is a trophy of grace throughout all eternity, he certainly can have peace. According to Ephesians 2:5, believers in Christ will be a living illustration throughout all eternity of what the grace of God can do.

The securing of the peace of God is more than an act of faith; it is a fruit of the Spirit. God Himself produces in us that wonderful experience of rest of heart. One cannot explain it, but one can enjoy and experience it.

THREEFOLD CONDITION OF PEACE

How can we get this peace? There are three simple rules. The peace of God must rest upon implicit faith. In Isaiah 26:3, a familiar verse to many, there is this promise: "Thou wilt keep him in perfect peace, whose mind is stayed on thee: because he trusteth in thee." When we lose this peace of God, it is always traceable to an imperfection in our faith. We have somehow taken our eyes off the Lord instead of trusting Him perfectly. We have begun to lean on the arm of flesh and to return to the principle that *we* have to do it, that it all depends on us. But how wonderful it is to rest: "Thou wilt keep him in perfect peace, whose mind is stayed on thee." This is one of the vital secrets of peace.

A second secret of peace in a practical way is prayer. In Philippians 4:6-7, a very familiar section, we read: "Be careful [or be anxious] for nothing; but in every thing by prayer and supplication with thanksgiving let your requests be made known unto God." Prayer is our part. In every circumstance, in everything, along with thanksgiving—the reminders of what God has done and is doing—"let your requests be made known unto God." The promise follows: "And the peace of God, which passeth all understanding, shall keep your hearts and minds through Christ Jesus." That is a wonderful promise. It is so complete. The heart of man, as we understand it in the Scripture, is the seat of our will, of our affection, emotion, attitudes, and love. We sometimes think our emotions are uncontrollable. God says He will keep our hearts at rest. But it also mentions our minds. Sometimes óur problems are intellectual problems. What shall I do with my business? With my job? What shall I do with this problem, or with that problem? Mental problems are often the cause of much trouble. God says, however, I will give peace there, too. If God takes the mind of man and the heart of man and gives peace in both, there is certainly peace complete. It is a promise, but it will not be accomplished simply through prayer. The Philippian passage states that peace comes "through Christ Jesus." When we have performed our part in prayer and in trust, God will undertake for us and give us this wonderful peace.

A third very simple rule is found in Colossians 3:15, "And let the peace of God rule in your hearts." It is a plain exhortation. It really is surprising, if we are willing to admit it, how some of us love to worry. If we did not have something to worry about, we would feel very unnatural. Some Christians are happy-go-lucky in their attitude toward the problems of life. Others may be inclined to be careful about everything. But this exhortation applies to all of us. "Let the peace of God rule." *Let it.* In other words, God wants to give us this gift of "my peace." He wants the Christian to have rest of heart. He wants us to experience that for which the heart of man naturally hungers. It is not for the apostles only. It is not for preachers, exclusively. It is for every trusting believer in Christ. Everyone who is willing to trust God and have peace with God through Jesus Christ can also have the peace of God.

It is rather a strange thing that we are willing to trust God for eternity, for heaven, for all the issues that stretch on as far as our mind can go. Many have no unrest of heart as far as eternal salvation is concerned and are perfectly satisfied that they have peace with God. But when it comes to thinking of ordinary, every-day problems, they cannot get rest of heart. We are willing to trust God for eternity, but when it comes to time we think we just have to worry along. Let us be reasonable. If God can save our souls and provide for us for all eternity, if He has manifested His love, His wisdom and His power unmistakably, the God of eternity is also the God of time, and he can give us peace.

The Scriptures are plain. God has never promised us an easy time in this life. Christ told His disciples, "In the world ye shall have tribulation." As far as we know, every one of the eleven faithful disciples died a martyr's death. The death of James is recorded. The deaths of Paul and Peter are predicted. Apparently, the others also died the death of a martyr. Is not this a pretty hard lot for those who had trusted Christ and had given their lives over to Him? "In the world ye shall have tribulation." Christ not only promised us tribulation, but He said: "Be of good cheer; I have overcome the world." "These things I have spoken unto you, that in me ye might have peace."

This is the peculiar characteristic of our Christian faith. In the midst of unrest, chaos, and uncertainty in a war-torn world, the Christian has the peace of heaven in his heart and in his daily experience. That is wonderful. In heaven we will have peace, and in heaven we will have rest of heart. But in heaven everyone will have peace. The marvelous thing now is that God has given us the opportunity of testifying to His wonderful grace in the midst of trouble, having in our hearts the peace of God that passeth all understanding.

Can we have peace in our time? The Scriptures teach that there can be no peace among the nations until Christ returns. He, the Prince of peace, will bring peace to the nations. But the Bible also teaches that here and now anyone who is willing to trust in Christ can have peace with God. Any Christian who is willing to let peace rule in His heart can have the wonderful peace of God.

There is an old saying, "The best way to avoid the shadows is to face the sun." If you are facing the sun you do not see the shadows. If you are facing the Son of God, if your face is fixed upon Him, you can have peace even though you are in trial.

Christ is our peace; Christ made peace for us; Christ gives His own peace. "Let not your heart be troubled." "My peace I give unto you."